Born in the USA, Susan Poole now lives in Cappoquin, Co. Waterford and is a full-time writer. She has written several Frommer Travel Guides and contributes to numerous newspapers and magazines. A recipient of the Lowell Thomas Travel Guide Award, she also writes fiction.

*To Margaret, with all the love in my heart,
and to Sarah, who found her when she was lost.*

One Sad Ungathered Rose

Susan Poole

The Collins Press

Published by The Collins Press, West Link Park, Doughcloyne, Wilton, Cork

British Library in cataloguing in Publication data.

Printed in by MPG Books Ltd.

Jacket by Raven Design

ISBN: 1-898256-62-4

Why this book?

Her name is Margaret.
She is schizophrenic.
And she is my daughter.

Her hospitalization record in New York while still in her twenties is impressive: Metropolitan Hospital twice; Payne Whitney Psychiatric Clinic once; Bellevue Hospital three times; Central Islip State Hospital once; Manhattan State Hospital twice; St Vincent's Hospital twice; and twice she was admitted to New Jersey hospitals, the details of which are lost in the confusion of her mind.

Between hospitalizations, she lived at home with me and her small daughter; dreary welfare hotels on Manhattan's Upper West Side, with various men who sheltered her briefly; and for months on end in a never-never land that left no record in her memory. In her thirties and into her late forties, she survived with only occasional hospitalizations, living for the most part on the streets of Austin and other Texas cities.

When schizophrenia strikes a family, no member escapes its fallout. A father, brother or sister may experience its heartbreak in widely differing manifestations and to varying degrees. But the bond between mother and child runs so deep and is so special that a mother's suffering is unique. There is the searing pain of seeing her child plunged into a strange, frightening 'reality' that is unlike any she has ever known and with which neither of them is equipped to cope. Inevitably, soul-destroying emotions and inner conflicts are set in motion that will be instantly recognizable to other mothers of schizophrenic children, but to few others.

This book is written for those countless mothers who, day in and day out, struggle desperately to find a way to live with the demons of schizophrenia. It is a lonely, bewildering world they inhabit, and I can only hope that these pages will bring them some degree of the understanding and comfort that for so long eluded me.

In her early teens Margaret began to slip away from me. Looking back, it was as though she had waded down a river-bank into the edges of a swift, strong current she was powerless to resist. For several years, that current was to swirl and eddy around her, hurling her far away from me, then suddenly sweeping her back to the closeness we knew before she became its victim. Those were the bittersweet times. Each time I held on to the belief that *this* time she was out of its grip forever. And each time, that powerful current would reach for her again, and she would be gone.

By the early 1980s it was as though that strong current of schizophrenia had taken Margaret far downstream, forever out of my life. Even the rare times we were together – separated by years, now, rather than months – she was a stranger to me, someone whose inner life I could not even imagine. When I did, on rare occasions, meet the people among whom she moved, they were nothing more than surface characters to me. They, like Margaret, lived shadowy secret lives that were beyond my comprehension.

The secret life that had become the centre of my daughter's

being did anything *but* provide a safe, happy environment for her. When, on a regular basis, she lost all touch with reality, her inner pain was often so intense that it manifested itself in physical symptoms. With every episode, my heart broke a little more. Each crisis threw me into a quagmire of uncertainty, as though I were lost in an alien land, one whose rules – whose very language – were unknown to me. Not once did a clear path open up to the right thing to do.

Early on, in a society that attached a deeply scarring stigma to any suggestion of mental illness, I found other names for what was wrong with my daughter. Looking back, I can see with vivid clarity the signs that should have signalled a much more serious condition than the teenage 'behaviour problems' to which I attributed them. Like most mothers, in the beginning I denied that schizophrenia was in any way applicable to *my* child. As for Margaret, herself, even to this day, she has not been able to acknowledge that she is a victim of the disease.

I had much to learn.

Schizophrenia is as old as the human race. It was not until the early 1900s that it was given an official name, a combination of the Greek *schizos* (split) and *phrenos* (the mind) which for many years led to a common misperception that confused it with multiple personality disorder. In truth, schizophrenia is a whirlwind of confusion – there simply is no succinct definition of the illness. A distorted view of reality, paranoia, delusions, disembodied voices, and an inability to integrate thoughts and feelings coherently all come and go in the schizophrenic's dreamlike world. Alarmingly, statistics show that 10% of all people with schizophrenia eventually commit suicide.

In its search for an underlying cause of this damnable disease, the medical profession has wandered through a maze of possibilities as perplexing as its symptoms. When Margaret was first diagnosed, the prevailing practice was to place blame on parents, more particularly on mothers. Psychoanalysis, psychosurgery (lobotomy) and drugs to correct chemical imbalances – each, in turn, has held the treatment spotlight.

In the United States, my native country, nearly four million people will at some time in their lives suffer from schizophrenia, with close to two million acutely ill at any given time. In Ireland, my home for many years now, the figure is between thirty-five and forty thousand. According to the Schizophrenia Association of Ireland, the figures rise to a minimum of 175,000 who are directly affected by the disease when families as well as patients are included.

For roughly 10% of schizophrenics, life is an unending nightmare. Until medical research finds the key to unlock their permanently clouded minds, full-time supervision is the only option. Another 25% will have no more than three or four psychotic breaks (a loss of all sense of reality) in a lifetime and with the help of modern medicines will be able to function more or less normally.

Somewhere between these two groups lies the other 65%, the chronically ill like my daughter. For them it is a different story. In the United States, until the late 1950s, most were institutionalized, with little hope of release even during their lucid periods. During the 1960s, the introduction of anti-psychotic drugs and the rising costs of custodial care led the mental health profession, with enormous public support, to embark on a programme of releasing patients like Margaret into the community. It was believed that they would be able to function normally for long periods *as long as medication was administered regularly*.

Certainly it seemed to be an enlightened way of dealing with schizophrenia, and a return to the old 'snakepit' institutions was unthinkable. In theory, it was a good plan, but its success depended heavily on adequate aftercare, and because that care was not provided, it failed miserably. Chiefly for economic reasons, community health care centres in America were charged with responsibility for released patients, but United States federal and state funds were forthcoming to establish only a bare minimum, and there was almost no provision for any other supervision. As a result, patients were hospitalized only when in the throes of an acute psychotic break, treated with drugs that returned them to a semblance of normality, and released to fend for themselves. Regular returns to the clinic were left solely to the patient's discretion.

To the disorientated minds of schizophrenics, the prospect of leaving a familiar room and travelling the streets for the outpatient care that was so vital was simply too fearful. Or they just forgot and did not show up for treatment. Without the continuity of medication, there was little hope that they could maintain stability. The relief programme was a disaster, and Margaret and I were among its victims. Her illness began in the late 1960s, when the programme was at the height of disarray, and little was done to improve the situation right through the 1970s and 1980s.

Since that time, many dedicated mental health professionals have made steady progress, but the sad fact is that a high percentage of schizophrenics fall through the cracks of the imperfect systems now in place. Modern psychiatry *does* recognize the mental patient's needs beyond hospital treatment, and outpatient clinics and therapy groups *do* exist at many psychiatric centres. In far too many cases, however, follow-up care is still woefully inadequate. Even though the mental health profession is recognising more and more the importance of providing consistent medication, a decent place to live, and day-time activity centres, relatively few schizophrenics receive such services.

Without that support, schizophrenics are lost. Within months – sometimes weeks – they are back in hospital, once more on the familiar treadmill of treatment, release and regression. Patients recovering from a psychotic break are still being released to live on their own, with no help through the traumatic transition and no supervision to be sure that medication continues to be taken regularly. Even as this is written, Margaret was recently hospitalized for a serious physical illness that her doctors insisted must be followed by a prolonged period of bed rest. The hospital released her with no follow-up support, even though she had no home to return to other than an abandoned car that she had made her home. It almost cost her her life.

Headlines, with sickening regularity, scream the deadly consequences of that kind of neglect. Yet public horror at terrible crimes committed by 'recently released mental patients' fades rapidly when it comes to correcting the inadequacies of treatment programmes. Virtually every attempt to establish supervised half-way houses that can mean salvation for those afflicted with schizophrenia is met with a resounding 'not in *my* backyard'.

There is no question that the social stigma with which I wrestled for so many years has lessened considerably over time. Mental and emotional disturbances more often elicit sympathy than instant condemnation these days. And to its credit, the medical profession is recognizing more and more that families of the mentally ill should be an integral part of their treatment. In Ireland, for example, there is a growing network of support groups for parents of schizophrenics. But there are still glaring instances of 'patient confidentiality' denying families any real understanding of mental illness and the part that they can play in counteracting its disastrous effects on parents and siblings, as well as on the patient.

There continues to be too little effort to help parents and other family members understand many of the known effects of the disease on schizophrenics. From the beginning of Margaret's illness, my own ignorance of very basic facts about what was happening to her – the acute increase in her hearing and visual sensations, for example – stood between me and any steps I might have taken to make her life more bearable. Had I known about these symptoms early on, my irritation when she insisted on turning the radio and television sound down to an almost inaudible level could have been replaced by understanding. Drawn curtains on bright, sunlit days would not have been a source of such annoyance to me. It was not until she was deep in the grip of schizophrenia that a psychiatric doctor took the time and trouble to give me this kind of practical insight.

There is no road map to guide a mother through the bewildering twists and turns of her schizophrenic child's inner world. She can only stand by and watch that child become more and more entangled in a web of madness that she is powerless to combat.

The story of my personal journey through that hellish landscape is a tragedy suffered by hundreds of thousands of mothers of schizophrenic offspring. A terrible pall of isolation and loneliness engulfs us, and inescapable fears, guilt pangs and the heartbreak of helplessness are common to us all.

So why write this book?

Though I readily recognize the cathartic benefits of committing my story to the printed page, it has been one of the most painful undertakings of my life. More than once as I wrote, I have yearned to put it all aside and just get on with my own life as best I can, a survival policy to which I have clung so many times in the past. Proverbial wisdom, however, has it that 'trouble shared is trouble halved', and I write in the certainty that there would have been great comfort for me during all those years just to know I was not alone in my grief. Living with the dreadful certainty that it was simply not within my power to protect my daughter from the ravages of her illness would have been easier if that sorrow, too, could have been shared. Nevertheless, when I got down to put my history into words, it was as though everyone concerned – both my daughters, other family members, members of the medical profession, etc. – sat on my shoulder and blocked out the candor and the honesty without which my writing would be worthless. It wasn't until I changed most of the names that I could write freely.

My older daughter, Elizabeth, who lived through many of the bad times with me and saw at first hand the changes in her sister, was enormously supportive. Other family members came to my rescue with practical help when I could not cope. They shared my pain and reached out with as much comfort as they could offer.

But I sorely needed the understanding of other mothers who were struggling with the same day-to-day futility that was engulfing me. They alone would know the heartbreak of having to view my lovely child not solely as a victim of a vicious disease, but also as my 'sad, ungathered rose', a poignant phrase Oliver Wendell Holmes penned about his spinster aunt, and one that captures for me the grief in my heart for the lost beauty of my child. They would know, too, the ripple effect of that heartbreak as I struggled to prevent real damage to my relationship with my older daughter and the healthy emotional development of Margaret's small child.

In my isolation, the journals I kept through the long years of Margaret's illness were the only safe haven for my anguish. Excerpts from those journals reflect the hurt, frustration and guilt that bedevilled me, but which I could confide nowhere else. Anger also shows through those pages: anger that at times reached rage proportions – rage against the disease that had claimed my daughter; my inability to deal with it; a mental health profession that failed me time after time when I sought help and guidance; and society's callous and indifferent attitudes toward mental or emotional illness.

The journals highlight a resentment that grew with every psychotic break, as I rushed to deal with yet another crisis – putting everything else on hold – only to be left heavily in debt, my own life in shambles, and in the end Margaret herself no better off.

Close on the heels of every other emotion came crushing assaults of guilt, which I am even now unable to ward off entirely. As the mental health profession moved more and more towards acknowledging that schizophrenia is a biological disease of the brain that has nothing to do with a mother's influence on her child, I tried to hold on to the dictum that 'I didn't cause it, and I can't cure it'. Intellectually, I accepted that without question. In my heart, I could not help but wonder.

In my upbringing it had been an underlying principle for parents that they must bear the ultimate responsibility for their children. Margaret was my child, and there was no escaping the conviction that it must have been something I did – or worse, did *not* do – that had brought her so much suffering. Was it *my* failure to teach her to cope with life as it really is that had brought her to such a state? No matter how many times I relived her growing up years, I could never unearth the roots of that failure; nor did I ever know how to go about repairing such dreadful damage.

This book, however, is in no sense a crusade for changes that will have to come if my personal story is not to be repeated. Nor is it a 'How to' manual for coping with the mental illness of a loved one. The journals, letters and experiences recorded here are not, and cannot be, anyone's story but my own. I make no claim of objectivity. I can, after all, inhabit only my own skin and emotions; I cannot get inside Margaret's mind or do justice to all the forces with which she has had to deal. Neither am I qualified to point the way to a realistic hope that schizophrenia will some day be eliminated from the catalogue of human illnesses.

In the final analysis, then, this book is simply my own story as it has been affected by my schizophrenic daughter.

Chapter One

10 August 1995

To Whom It May Concern

I am trying to locate an author who has published several travel books in the recent past using the Frommer Guide title. I believe they were concerning New Orleans and New Zealand.

I work with the homeless and I am trying to find her for her daughter, who is very ill. She has lost contact with her mother and would very much like to contact her again before it is too late.

I will greatly appreciate any help you can offer me in this matter.

Sincerely,
Sarah McCoy

Eight years. Eight years of silence. Eight years of emotional pain that haunted my every waking hour. Even when my conscious thoughts were not taken up with the hurt, it lay there just below the surface, ready to engulf me at the simplest incident or observation. Eight years of searching the face of every homeless person I passed on the street, of wondering if Margaret were still wandering the streets, homeless. Eight years of reading everything about schizophrenia I could get my hands on, searching for understanding.

And now I had this letter, albeit fifteen days after it was written. The wonder is that it reached me at all. I had moved twice since I last saw Margaret, and now live in Ireland, so the Manhattan address she had for me was long obsolete. All my efforts to find her before each move had proved fruitless.

I sat staring at the letter, and as I reread it, my world once more tumbled upside down. Suppose Margaret was already dead? Where was the strong maternal instinct I had always believed would tell me if that were so? Obliterated by those eight years of silence?

If she was still alive, did I really *want* to contact her? Awful thought! Surely the pure joy of finding her again should be enough to banish all those painful memories.

But it wasn't.

As powerful as is motherly love, it had failed to protect Margaret in the past. Would it be any different this time? What could have happened to alter the hard fact that there was little or nothing I could do for her? Could I once more strain my fragile finances to the breaking point and beyond, when a hurry-up dash across the Atlantic and halfway across America might well be as futile as every such rescue attempt in the past? Was I willing – or able – to take all that on again?

Through all the sadness of those eight years, I had worked hard to grow scar tissue over the wounds left by devastating hurt and anger, and I had learned to get on with my own life. In an instant, this letter ripped apart those carefully cultivated scars. Would the gaping wounds, as fresh and as painful now as when newly inflicted, wipe away the contentment I had found in Ireland?

And what about Jenny, Margaret's daughter?

Did this letter pose a threat not only to me, but an even more dangerous threat to her? Had I the right to land this on her again? At the age of thirty, she had made for herself a life that was safe and happy. Did I have the right *not* to tell her? From the time Jenny had first come to live with me at the age of three, I had never concealed her mother's illness from her. Even as a young child, in her straightforward way, she was able to see things just as they were and accept that they might never be as we both wished they could be. Her innocent honesty had, in fact, sustained me through many a crisis.

Jenny had grown into a lovely woman, filled with compassion for others, always conscious of her mother's tragedy. I knew that she and her husband, Seán, had a strong, solid love that would see Jenny through whatever emotional turmoil this letter carried with it. But what of their two little daughters? What effect would this contact with their grandmother have on them, now or in later years? Surely, *they* should not have to deal with all the worries, sadness and potential catastrophe that I knew might lie ahead.

There was another worry. Jenny and Seán had long planned to have one more child to complete their family, and Jenny was now in the very early stages of the pregnancy they had longed for. I was worried about her making such a strenuous trip – she had lost one of a set of twins just a week or so before, and if the remaining foetus was to survive, she would have to avoid stress and fatigue, which would be impossible if she were to undertake this trip. She was already bleeding, which the doctor felt was not a good sign. It was no good talking to her, however; she was determined to go, and felt strongly that this might be the last time she would see her mother. I would just have to try and see that she looked after herself as much as possible.

How on earth could I protect that family that was so precious to me? I knew at once that I could not.

Could Jenny and I once more summon the courage to cope with this renewed close contact with Margaret's illness? Would

Jenny be able to find her own way to protect her loved ones? As my numbed mind struggled to deal with this new development, panic set in, led by an almost forgotten, but instantly familiar, sense of isolation.

From a financial point of view, this couldn't have come at a worse time. Already, I was well into a substantial overdraft, with no sight of money from a book contract or any other lump sum payment to help bring things back to a solvent basis. For the foreseeable future, there was only my Social Security cheque of $620 a month, which translated into only a little over half of that in Irish punts – barely enough to cover my living expenses. This would be a horribly expensive trip, and I would have to use credit cards as well as looking to Michael for at least a part of the expenses. Would I *never* be free of financial worries, I wondered.

When Jenny and I rang the telephone number in the letter, Sarah McCoy turned out to be an Emergency Room technician in one of the largest hospitals in Austin, Texas. She had taken an interest in Margaret during one of her previous hospitalizations and had kept in touch with her between illnesses. She told us that Margaret had been living on the streets of Austin for most of the eight years she had been lost to us. I was surprised to learn that my search for her through social agencies in that city had been futile simply because during all those Austin years she had resumed using my second husband's surname, even though the name itself must have awakened painful memories for her. I had to wonder if her deep yearning for family life had led her to romanticize our years when there was a father figure in our home, no matter how unsatisfactory he had been.

This latest hospitalization, Sarah said, was for a G.I. bleed. 'That means serious internal bleeding', she explained. 'Her liver is almost gone, and she has severe pancreas damage, as well as advanced emphysema. They are irreversible conditions, but she is taking medication that could keep them from worsening. It's expensive, but she gets it through welfare.'

Incredibly, Margaret was again back on the streets. Having stopped the bleeding, the attending doctor had stressed that she must have complete bed rest for the foreseeable future. The hospital, however, had discharged her in the full knowledge that she had no place to go but the abandoned car behind a field of junk cars that had been her only home for years.

Bed rest on the streets? A contradiction.

Indignation swept over me like a white-hot flame. How could that possibly have happened? It was the same old bureaucratic story. If social service agencies were not already involved, no one took the responsibility for letting them know that there was a need. And if a welfare agency had been paying for her medication, why did they not follow up on her living conditions? The situation reflected a dismissive, uncaring attitude that had become so familiar in the past when I looked for help for Margaret and which I had almost forgotten over the years of her absence.

'Surely someone could have done something to get her off the streets,' I seethed aloud to Jenny.

'But, Granny,' she put her arms around me, 'just remember how many times we tried our best to keep her with us and couldn't. Maybe someone like this Sarah McCoy *did* offer her a place to stay and she just wouldn't accept it.'

The fact remained: Margaret was once more homeless, and I knew I would have to go to her. 'One way or another,' I told Jenny, 'I'll work out how we can pay for the trip. Maybe we can leave the day after tomorrow.'

'No, Granny, we have to go *now*. We can't wait another day. She might be dead by then.' Her voice broke, and I was struck by the depth of sadness she had carried with her over the years. 'It's been twelve years since I've seen my mother, and this might be the last chance I'll have. We have to go tomorrow.' Jenny had been in Ireland during her mother's last two visits to New York. What a long wait it had been for her! It was my turn to hug and reassure her.

By using a combination of credit cards, I could just manage our airfares one way. I made the bookings. The return fare would just have to take care of itself.

As has been true in every emergency I can remember, my hair was dirty and most of the clothes I would need were in the laundry basket. The night flew by as I shampooed my hair, washed the clothes and tried to think what I would need to pack. Maybe, I smiled at the thought, if I could just manage to keep my hair and clothes clean, all those emergencies might never happen at all!

Incredibly, less than twenty-four hours after I opened that letter, we were on our way to Austin. God alone knew what lay ahead, and maybe He wasn't too sure.

I had a strong, almost eerie, sense of unreality as the plane took off. Still, my husband Michael would be waiting for us between planes in New York. Our private joke was that we were currently enjoying a 'commuting marriage', since it would be another six months before he reached retirement age and could join me in Ireland. Now he would be a bulwark of protection against the threat that permeated what should have been a purely joyful reunion with my long-lost daughter.

Jenny and I chatted about everything under the sun during the six-hour flight from Ireland to New York, always coming back to what we were flying toward. I must have said at least a dozen times, with no notion that I was repeating myself, 'I am scared to death. I've forgotten how awful it is not to know what to do or say. Suppose I put a foot desperately wrong?' All those years, and I still had not learned how to respond to Margaret's illness.

Jenny was waging her own battle against bitterness and guilt. Seán had insisted that she use the family's holiday money for this trip, and she told me, 'What am I *doing*? This is my *mother*! She walked away from me, and hasn't made any attempt to see me in twelve years, and I am taking away their holiday from Seán and the girls.' I knew she was also wrestling with the uncertainty of what her mother's re-entrance into her life could do to her family.

I also knew that Jenny and I must talk about what we could

and could not do for her mother. So many times in the past we had brought her home to recover. Now, despite all the dangers, our first impulse would almost certainly be to bring her back to Ireland. But I also recognized that, this time, it really wasn't going to be possible, for a lot of reasons. Best if we acknowledged that from the start. We both knew there was no help we could give to Margaret in Ireland. She would not be eligible for social benefits there, and if she walked away from us, she would be in a strange country. To my surprise, Jenny had already thought that through and knew it would not work.

It was a time out of time for us both. Six hours that moved us closer to an uncertain present and future. Six hours filled with memories of how it had all begun and all that had followed.

Chapter Two

18 March 1961
For the third night in a row, Margaret has come home after midnight. Where does she go? Not for one minute can I believe her story that she was studying at a friend's house until that late hour. She puffs up with righteous indignation when I question her, and I just don't have the nerve to call around trying to find her. If this is what she's like at thirteen, how am I going to manage through the rest of her teen years? So far, there are no real problems with Elizabeth [my other daughter, four years older than Margaret], but something is badly amiss with Margaret.

I have no idea how to handle this, and I have a strong sense that she is slipping away from me. I have always felt such a special closeness with both my girls. Why is that changing with Margaret? Can it be that after all this time she is just now feeling the effect of Paul's [my first husband and father of both daughters] leaving us and our breakup with Sam [my second husband, stepfather to the girls]? She was only an infant when

Paul left us, and I cannot believe she has even hazy memories of him. As for Sam, Margaret and Elizabeth were both obviously relieved when we made the joint decision to divorce him. Is this a delayed reaction to that decision? Maybe all the experts are right and the girls do need a father, no matter how bad he might be. Don't know what I can do about it at this point, so guess I'll just muddle through as best I can.

'Muddling through' wasn't really my style. All my life, I had taken pride in an ability to take decisive action in almost any set of circumstances. I held firmly to the creed that 'If something is wrong, you fix it'. So, when I fell in love with Paul, what in today's world would have been an affair based on not much more than a strong sexual attraction, became a marriage. Back then, 'nice' girls did not have affairs, so I had 'fixed it' by marrying him in 1943, just after my seventeenth birthday. In only a few months he was in Europe on active Second World War duty.

Elizabeth was born in 1944, when Paul was in the midst of fierce fighting in France. I was overjoyed when he returned in 1947 and we could begin a real family life. Paul's carefree, happy-go-lucky nature had attracted me from the time we met, but that same nature and our mutual youth and inexperience made it difficult for him to assume the responsibilities of a wife and child. He struggled valiantly for almost a year, but Margaret's arrival in 1948 was the final straw. He simply walked away.

Left at the age of twenty-two, with two small children to raise on my own, I arranged care for the girls and spent a year at the University of North Carolina studying secretarial science which would equip me with the necessary skills to earn a living. It was one of the longest years of my life, but at its end I was able to find work and make a home for my children in Raleigh, North Carolina.

Elizabeth was a bright, articulate child with an inquiring mind. She revelled in sharing with me her excitement at all the things she was learning in school, as well her enthusiasm for music and her budding talent as a painter. Margaret was a cheerful, sensitive girl who exuded an almost palpable sweetness that instinctively drew people to her. Often she came running in with a handful of wild flowers, or just plain weeds – a present for me because she knew I would see their beauty, as *she* did. Indeed, she showed an acute appreciation for natural beauty in almost any form, be it cows and horses in a field on Sunday drives through the North Carolina countryside or tiny city gardens in Raleigh.

Paul dropped out of sight and made no effort to keep in touch with us. I made an extra effort to stay close to Margaret and Elizabeth and kept a close watch for signs of any emotional hurt they might feel about his indifference. As far as I could tell, however, the loss of their father was inflicting no serious damage to either of my daughters.

The only cloud on our horizon was the constant financial struggle – in our straitened circumstances, even the occasional ice cream cone became a luxury. After five years of grappling with an inadequate income, I was introduced to Sam by mutual friends. I was then twenty-seven years old, and he was in his mid-forties. In spite of the age difference, when he proposed in 1953 I accepted with a great sigh of relief, even though it meant moving to Birmingham, Alabama, where he and his brother owned two chemist shops. Here, at last, was security – not the best motive for marriage, and as it turned out, a terrible mistake.

In my yearning to escape from financial woes, I had failed to recognize Sam's miserly character. It quickly revealed itself as he doled out money for each household expense, requiring me to account for every penny. When I asked for an allowance so that I could manage our everyday expenses, it was instantly denied. Every purchase for the girls' clothing had to be justified before money could be spent. Even more damaging was his ability to squelch the girls' budding interest in school or social activities. His vision of family life was one of spirit-killing discipline and tight-fisted financial control.

Eventually I went back to work to pay for the ballet lessons Margaret had her heart set on, as well as Elizabeth's coveted horseriding instruction. Try as I might, however, I was never able to counteract the devastating emotional impact Sam's mean-spiritedness was having on me and my daughters. They no longer shared openly with me their spontaneous joy in simple pleasures, and I could see both girls drawing inward.

By 1960 it was clear to me that our home situation had deteriorated beyond repair. Ending the marriage, however, meant that the girls would once more be deprived of a father figure, and I was far from sure that would be fair to them. When I sat down with Elizabeth, then sixteen, and Margaret, twelve, to discuss the possibility of leaving Sam, to my surprise their only reaction was one of relief. Together, we made the decision to leave, and we moved into an apartment across town. By this time, my work as executive assistant to the president of an insurance company paid enough to support us comfortably.

Both girls were thrilled when my mother and father drove up from Florida to take them back for a summer at the beach and give me time to attend to the finalization of the divorce and get our new apartment in order.

Dear daughter, [Note: All my life, my father addressed his correspondence to me in this rather courtly style]

We arrived last night about 9:45 after a pleasant drive home. Margaret and Elizabeth seem happy to spend this time with us, and Mother and I are convinced that after the proceedings are over and you and the girls get settled you all three will be much happier. We feel sure that you can and will make a go of raising your girls alone. They both seem concerned over what has happened and what effect it will have on you, but they both are equally sure that you are doing the right thing and are more than willing to do their part in seeing that you three do get along, not only satisfactorily, but much more happily than any of you have been the past few years.

They are mighty precious girls, and I know they will help you all they can in the future. Don't worry about them, just concentrate on the job you have to do to continue being able to care for yourself and your family, remembering always that Mother and I are with you 100%.

Love,
Daddy

I have reread this undated letter from my father many times over the years since, especially during periods of agonizing self-doubt. My parents' faith in me never failed to provide the support I needed in whatever crisis reared its head.

Once more, the girls and I were on our own, but laughter was back in our lives, and I treasured our regained warm, close relationship. We all felt a great sense of freedom, and when the usual parent/child conflicts arose, such as curfew times when they were out at night, Elizabeth and Margaret both were content to accept my rulings.

When the change in Margaret's behaviour began, the pattern of one deception after another came as a shock, and I did not know how to handle it. I had to wonder if she needed a stronger hand than mine.

For the first time, 'muddling through' was replacing an inborn and unwavering confidence in my ability to provide a good, sound upbringing for Margaret. I spent hours defending to myself the decision to deprive her of a father figure. The lifelong credo that had always served me so well simply did not apply. Something was terribly wrong, and there didn't seem to be any way that I could fix it.

10 May 1961

My life is fast turning into a nightmare. I am reeling from a series of little shocks that make it terribly clear Margaret has a secret life that she has no intention of sharing with me. Over the last month or two, she has several times rung me at the office after school to say that she was spending the afternoon with one of her schoolmates. And time after time I have accidentally discovered that she was some place else. The worst of it is that she steadfastly sticks to her story no matter how obvious it is that she is lying. She is shutting me out entirely from her private world, and I have to fight huge waves of panic. School holidays are right around the corner – what am I going to do then?

In my ignorance and bewilderment, I treated all these incidents as nothing more than behaviour problems, a form of teenage rebellion. As for the changes in Margaret's appearance – heavy, near grotesque eye and lip make-up and revealing, bare-midriff fashions – I saw them as no more than a passing phase. She will grow out of all this, I kept telling myself, and I resolved to try and keep my composure and just get her safely through this period that was so upsetting to me. When the possibility of boarding school arose, I felt that if she were in a safe environment, away from her circle of undesirable friends, the real Margaret would surface. Recommended by a friend, a Quaker boarding school in the little town of Friendsville, set in a lovely Tennessee valley, looked like the perfect answer.

4 September 1961

Well, it's done – Margaret is safely (I hope!) ensconced in Friendsville Academy. Never thought I would be sending either of my girls off to boarding school, but this may be the very thing we all need. She seems to like her roommate and really turned on the charm for the principal when he met us. Fingers crossed that the Quaker code of good behaviour and the supervision of those kindly people will straighten her out – Lord knows, I haven't been able to.

Elizabeth and I got back home in the wee hours and fell into bed, exhausted after the long drive from Birmingham up to Tennessee and back. In spite of sleeping like a log until nearly noon today, I am still bone weary. But what a relief to turn over some of my responsibility for Margaret to someone else. One thing is sure, I will sleep with an easy mind tonight!

Sadly, it didn't work.

Margaret made it clear that she did not really want to leave home, but in the end she seemed cheerful enough. For the first few weeks, she charmed the staff into thinking that she was a model student. They soon discovered, however, that from the very beginning she had been slipping out at night to go into the village, sometimes not returning until daylight. They suspected she had been drinking in the local beer parlour. Worst of all, she had enticed her roommate to go along. After the Christmas holidays, the school refused to take her back.

As before, what seemed to me like her heartfelt contrition led me to accept her own version of events – that she had only followed her roommate's lead. She was overjoyed at being home again and promised she would be no trouble now that she was back with Elizabeth and me.

5 June 1962, 2 a.m.

No hope of sleep this night. What an awful day! At my wit's end, I finally called the police and reported Margaret missing. She has been gone for two days and nights, and none of her school friends know where she is. Or if they do, they aren't going to tell me. Do all teenagers, I wonder, consider parents their enemy? What a shock when the police called me at the office late this afternoon to say Margaret is being held in the Juvenile Detention Centre. She was with a gang of delinquent boys when they were picked up on suspicion of car theft. She apparently is not implicated and can be released in my custody.

The Detention Centre was a madhouse – police and juvenile court workers trying to deal with a swarm of shouting parents, all demanding their children's release. It took all the courage I could muster to work my way through that mob to reach the desk of the clerks who could arrange Margaret's release. They must have been driven to distraction by the sheer numbers and hostility of parents vying for their attention, and yet they seemed quite casual, as if they were bored with the whole scene. Damn it, they weren't taking Margaret's situation seriously – they just didn't care about the trouble she is in. To my shame, I shouted at the woman across the desk, trying to

shake her out of that callousness I found so offensive. I know
her attitude must be unavoidable when she faces this sort of
crowd day in and day out, but this is my child, and someone
has to care.

When the clerk heard my name, she said the judge wanted to
see me and told me to wait in a tiny shoebox of a room behind
her desk. I panicked at the thought that the police must have got
it wrong and Margaret is involved in something unlawful.

When Judge Robins finally came in, he explained that Mr
Carter [the man for whom I worked] is a friend and had called
to tell him I was on my way to the Centre. Margaret is free to
go, he told me, but he thinks I should leave her in the Centre
overnight. He thinks it will teach her a lesson. Everything in
me rebels at the thought of leaving my child in such a place,
even for one night – she isn't like all those others. But I have to
admit I'm not doing too good a job with her on my own, and
this man must have years of experience with teenagers, so in
the end I agreed. When I asked if I could see Margaret and let
her know I will come for her tomorrow, he didn't think that was
wise. He did walk with me down a long corridor to where I
could see her at a distance. She's in a large barred room (he
called it a holding pen) filled with the roughest-looking teenage
girls I've ever seen. She looks dreadful – I don't think she has
washed her face and changed that awful make-up since she left
home, and there is a ragged look to her. She must feel totally
abandoned, and it was all I could do not to rush to her and
insist on her release then and there.

Tonight, I feel as though someone has used me for a
punching bag, physically sore all over. It will be a long, long
night, and I can only wait for daylight to come so I can bring
my daughter home. What I will do then, God only knows.

At the Detention Centre the next morning there was a note
asking me to see Judge Robins in his chambers. He took a
special interest in Margaret after Mr Carter had again telephoned to tell him of my distress.

In a way it was a comfort to talk to someone else about my problems with Margaret, but at the same time I wanted desperately to protect her from the judgements of this court official, a man who did not know her as I did, who could not see that this was not the *real* Margaret. I glossed over the previous few months, treating her conduct as an aberration. Foolishly, I clung to my pride and stubbornly refused to face simple truths. That first encounter with professional help set a pattern that was to take me years to overcome.

Judge Robins was a kindly man at heart, and I believe he felt deeply for me and for Margaret, but the advice he gave me only reinforced my denial of anything more serious than behaviour problems.

'Do you know she has been drinking?' he asked. That would explain, I thought, why she has been staying away at night. 'There is some suggestion that she may have taken drugs as well. You are lucky to find out about her use of alcohol and drugs at an early stage.' *Lucky?* Never in my life had I felt so *unlucky*.

'Have you thought that she may simply need a two-parent family, one with a strong father figure?' was his next question, and I had to confess I had been wrestling with that very thought for several months, but could not see any possibility of providing it for her. For the first time, I felt a flicker of hope when he suggested that my own parents, who lived in Florida, might take her in for the next school term. If they agreed, he felt my father's influence might well be the making of Margaret.

My own feelings were mixed. I was truly blessed in the parents I had been given, but I felt they did not deserve to have my problems dumped on their shoulders. Mother was finishing the last few years of her teaching career. My father, whose work for a number of Southern newspapers had given my two sisters and I an exciting childhood sparked with many moves from town to town, was now retired, and he had a serious heart condition.

In my eyes, my parents were as nearly perfect as anyone could be. There had been a great sense of fun in my growing up years, and both my mother and father had guided my sisters and I in our formative thinking, never imposing iron-clad principles, but gently pointing our own thoughts to positive and constructive conclusions. The closest I ever heard either of them come to passing judgement was Mother's mantra, 'Do *you* think that is really worthy of you?' They had given me high standards and then made me judge and jury of my own actions, imparting a tremendous sense of self-worth, which I so sorely wished for Margaret.

As an adult, I could always count on their love and support through all sorts of crises, yet they had also fostered a strong strain of independence in each of their daughters. That very quality had, I am certain, kept me from letting them know of this troubling time with Margaret. I just did not want them to know how terribly I was failing as a mother. Still, in truth, it was the only source of real help on my horizon at that moment. I decided that for Margaret's sake I was obliged to talk to my parents about her.

Unlike Judge Robins, they *did* know Margaret and loved her as I did, and both my girls adored their grandparents. What a relief it would be to have their help.

The next day, Margaret was tearful and contrite when I brought her home, insisting that she had been talked into joining the gang of boys in two days of wild escapades that ended in their stealing a car for a reckless drive through the streets of Birmingham. They had 'camped out' in the home of a young couple living together in a very rough neighborhood and who were reputed to be engaged in teenage prostitution. The boys had been drinking, but Margaret was adamant that she had drunk only soft drinks. Over and over, she protested her love for me and her regret at causing me so much worry. This was the Margaret I knew, and the warm glow of closeness was rekindled as we went home. There was no hint of resentment at having been left in detention overnight – one more example of her ability to say what I wanted to hear so convincingly that I was blinded to her true emotions. It would be years later that her bitter sense of abandonment surfaced in a savage barrage of verbal abuse.

6 June 1962

A long telephone talk tonight with Mother and Daddy. They are sympathetic about Margaret's problems and they feel, as I do, that this is nothing more than a difficult teenage period. I told them she had fallen in with a bad crowd, but I could not bring myself to tell them about the drinking and the possibility of drugs. After all, even though Judge Robins said there was no doubt about the drinking, he could be wrong, and I have to take Margaret's word. Anyway, it's no use worrying Mother and Daddy about that. Bless them, they were quick to say she can go to Mother's school next term, and Mother is going to set in motion transfer of Margaret's school records. But I cannot escape the unsettling suspicion that I am shifting to them a responsibility that is really mine.

Elizabeth graduates from high school next week, and Margaret's school term ends on the same day, so Mother and Daddy want both girls to come down for the holidays. Margaret loves the beach, and they think they can ease her into the idea of staying on for the school year. We have agreed to mention only the three months' holiday to her at this time. The main thing is to get her away from this crowd she's been running with.

It seemed just the right solution for Margaret and for me. My parents were more than willing to have her for the time being, and although her letters were full of homesickness, Margaret appeared to settle into the new school smoothly. In September, Elizabeth entered Birmingham Southern College. The year ahead promised to be a peaceful one, but it wasn't to be.

The first sign of trouble came in late November when Margaret had what Mother thought was a fainting spell. At the hospital, however, doctors discovered that she had overdosed on some of my father's pain-killing drugs, which she had stolen from an unlocked medicine chest. In spite of their shock, both my parents were touched by Margaret's penitent protestations and wanted to keep her with them, albeit now with a lock on the medicine chest.

In spite of my misgivings, I still was unable to look squarely at the pattern of deceit that was beginning to emerge. When Elizabeth and I drove down to Florida for the Christmas holidays, Margaret's contrite demeanour quickly laid to rest my lingering doubts, and it was agreed she would stay in Florida.

The holidays were hardly over, though, before Margaret was lying to my parents about her after-school activities. She was again wearing the heavy make-up and scanty outfits that caused us all great distress and was a sure signal that all was not well. Nevertheless, both my parents felt she should finish out the school year with them. As for Margaret, she embarked on a persistent campaign to drop out of school and come back home. Somehow, we managed to keep her in school until June, when she returned to Birmingham, and in September she enrolled in a school for beauticians that did not require a high school diploma.

I was not happy about her leaving high school at the age of fourteen, but again I was lulled into thinking that she was settling down and had a clear view of what she wanted to do with her life. Her school course was to run for two years, which would leave her equipped with a marketable skill at sixteen. To my disappointment, it was the same old story. Increasingly, she was absent from home for days on end, telling me she was staying with friends from the school, none of whom I ever met.

In November 1964 Margaret tearfully announced that she was pregnant. She had met George, a handsome, hard-living truck driver, at one of the bars she frequented where they turned a blind eye to underage drinkers. Although she was just a few months away from qualifying for certification, she dropped out of beautician school and she and George were married before the end of the month. Before Christmas, they had moved to Houston, Texas.

Would she be safe? I didn't know. George was more than ten years older than Margaret and a heavy drinker. He seemed an unlikely candidate for the father figure for which she might be subconsciously searching. On the other hand, he was apparently well able financially to take care of Margaret and the baby, and having a family might well change his lifestyle. I settled into an uneasy acceptance of the path her life was taking.

Elizabeth, having decided to take a year out of college, was living with my sister Louise, two years younger than I, and her family in New Jersey and had found a good job. For the first time in my adult life, I was on my own.

After my breakup with Sam I lost contact with many of our mutual friends, and with both my daughters living elsewhere, Birmingham was a lonely place. Impulsively, I plucked up my courage and flew to New York City in February 1965 and in one day found a high-paying job as executive secretary and office manager for Dr Martin Cherkasky, Director of a hospital in the Bronx. The city was more than a bit daunting, but my spirits soared as I flew back to Birmingham for my belongings and made a move that was to change my life.

In July of that same year, I celebrated becoming a grand-mother when George telephoned to tell me that Margaret had given birth to a daughter, Jenny. Earlier that year, Elizabeth had met and fallen in love with Kurt, a bright young German immigrant who was steadily progressing in his travel agency position. In August 1965 they were married in a small chapel near my Gramercy Park apartment.

1 September 1965

It is strange to sit here tonight and know that both my girls are now launched on lives they have chosen for themselves. I don't really worry about Elizabeth – Kurt is a lovely young man and they seem well suited. I am glad they will be living in Manhattan – it would be hard to have her far away, as Margaret is. As for Margaret, I am holding my breath. She, George and little Jenny are living in a tiny, scorching hot upstairs flat in Houston, and some of her letters seem to me to reflect a hint of her old distresses. There is almost always a mention of drinking, either at home or in neighbourhood bars with George. I don't read in those letters the joy and sense of responsibility I had hoped the new baby would give her. Nothing I can do from this distance, and truth to tell, I never was able to give her whatever it is she needed, even when she lived with me.

Strange, too, to think that now I am free to make a new life for myself. New York is an extraordinarily happy place for me, and I cannot help but wonder – where else will this new life take me?

Chapter Three

My work with Dr Cherkasky, one of the framers of the federal Medicare programme, turned out to be even more stimulating than I had initially thought it would be. Every day I learned something new, and medical people of national prominence passed through our office regularly. My personal horizon was expanding rapidly.

Early on in that first year in New York City, I met Michael. He worked at the Federal Reserve Bank in downtown New York, and although he commuted daily from his family home in nearby New Jersey, he spent most of his free time in New York and knew all sections of the city well. We spent almost every weekend together exploring its many faces, and it wasn't long before we fell in love. After so many years of struggling with family responsibilities, I was having the time of my life, with a sense of personal freedom that was new to me.

Perhaps because of my happiness, I failed to hear warning bells when Margaret rang to tell me she and Jenny were moving to a small town in Alabama to live with George's family, leaving him to work in Houston. She and George had financial troubles, she told me, and the move seemed like a sensible one. He would come for them after he had cleared some bills. I later discovered that she and George were on the verge of splitting up and both were drinking heavily. The baby had brought no change in their lifestyle, and they could not cope with family responsibilities.

Anxious to see Margaret again and to meet my first grandchild, I flew to Alabama, during the Christmas holidays – and ran head on into the truth of my daughter's condition. When I arrived at George's family home, Lillian, George's mother, told me that Margaret was working in the local pharmacy, leaving the baby with her during the day. Little Jenny won my heart at first sight, and it seemed a good sign that Margaret had a job, an indication that she was settling down. Or so I thought.

The shock came when I walked into the pharmacy and asked a young woman if I could see Margaret. 'Mama,' she laughed, 'don't you know me?'

I didn't. It was a long moment before I could detect my daughter in the apparition across the counter – her dark hair was bleached a brassy blond, her make-up was grotesque, her figure little more than skin and bones, her voice a high-pitched falsetto. She was, in fact, the very embodiment of drug addicts that up to then I had known only from television images. In a wounding flash, I saw clearly her reason for working where drugs were freely available.

Margaret insisted that her weight loss was the result of dieting and that she was not taking drugs. 'What do I need a doctor for? Mama, you know me, I would *never* take drugs.' Always I had accepted without question Margaret's version of events. Not so now. The evidence was far too clear – all the physical signs in her eyes, her skeletal form, and in her voice.

But George's mother backed up Margaret's story, insisting that she and Jenny were getting along 'fine' and that things would 'work out' between Margaret and George when he came to take them back to Texas. As for Margaret's continued drinking, it was a normal part of their family's household routine, and although she did admit that 'Margaret can match any man beer for beer', she could see no harm in it.

I could find no way to reach Margaret and get her to the help she so obviously needed. Jenny apparently was in good hands for the time being, but I had serious doubts that Margaret could survive the life she was leading. The very sight of my daughter was too painful to endure for even a day longer, and after a sleepless night confronting utter helplessness, I cut short my visit.

For years on end afterwards I was to wonder if this was my first mistake. Should I have stayed on and fought longer and harder to break through to my daughter, found some way to rescue her from certain disaster?

Weekends with Michael were a lifesaver, and as a closeness developed between us, I talked to him about Margaret, even though he had not met her. He listened sympathetically enough, but he was dismissive of my worries about a grown daughter who had become 'a drunk and a junkie' and had little hope of recovery. Every protective instinct in me rose in protest at his judgement of Margaret. It was my first brush with an insensitivity that would become agonizingly familiar in the years to come. I could not know then that Michael's understanding would grow over the years ahead, and that eventually his unwavering support would see me through crisis after crisis.

Elizabeth would understand and share my concerns, I knew, but she and Kurt were blissfully happy after the birth of their first child, Jane. How could I intrude on their joy? I felt desperately alone, and no matter how frequently I talked to Margaret by telephone, worry for her permeated everything else.

25 January 1967
Margaret and George have divorced, and she rang early this morning to ask if she and Jenny could come to New York to be with me. No money, of course, so I left work and wired her the airfare to fly up tomorrow. The thought of the three of us

squashed into my little flat brought on an attack of sheer panic. How on earth will I cope, especially if she is still drinking and taking drugs? A call from Louise [my sister, two years younger than I] took care of the most immediate of my worries – she and Daniel [Louise's husband] want Margaret and Jenny to come and live with them in Wayne [in New Jersey, only a few miles from New York City]. Their house is certainly big enough, and Louise insists that Margaret will be a big help with their five children. And she will love having a small child in the house. I had to tell Louise about Margaret's drinking, but said nothing about drugs. Louise feels that if Margaret is still drinking heavily, she and Daniel may be in a better position to help her than I can by myself. With all my heart, I hope so! If they can straighten Margaret out, I suppose that is justification enough for once more handing over my own responsibilities, but guilt is already beginning to set in.

Bless my family – first Mother and Daddy, and now Louise and Daniel are there when I need them most. Guilt or no guilt, I am really grateful for them.

Instead of sinking into restful sleep that night, I tossed and turned until daylight. My sister and her husband would welcome Margaret and her baby with nothing but love, and perhaps Daniel would turn out to be the strong father figure lacking in her life for so long. Why couldn't I rest easy? Try as I might, I could not erase the image of my daughter when I had last seen her in Alabama. Something deep inside me feared that, except for Jenny, Margaret would bring nothing but trouble with her.

When Louise and I met her plane the next evening, my heart sank. If anything, Margaret looked worse than when she had in Alabama. Not yet nineteen years old, she looked forty. 'Never mind,' Louise comforted me, 'she'll be a different girl when she settles into a stable family.' She was so confident and Margaret seemed so happy to see us both, that for the umpteenth time my fears were put to rest.

Indeed, over the next few months, life took on an almost idyllic routine, and I began to believe that the bad times might truly be in the past. Margaret was regaining her normal weight and her natural beauty was beginning to emerge as she softened her make-up. Jenny was a delight. The three of us spent most weekends together, either in New York or in Wayne. Michael shared our New York weekends, and Elizabeth and Kurt, now living in a small New Jersey township not far from the city, often brought Jane in to join us for a Sunday in Central Park.

It was good to see my daughters so settled, and I relaxed into the joys of being a grandmother and having my family close at hand. Best of all, my hopes for a happy life for Margaret were at an all-time high.

5 June 1967

I should have known it was too good to last. Louise came into the city tonight for a long talk about Margaret. She is drinking again – if she ever stopped. She gets very upset when Daniel tries to talk to her, and Louise decided to keep their liquor cabinet locked. Margaret apparently found the key rather easily, however, and has been taking bottles of whisky up to her room and drinking alone. Sometimes, even when they can't be sure she has been drinking, her behaviour is so odd it creates an awkward tension in the house. 'There are times,' Louise said, 'when I don't think she even hears us when we speak to her. She seems to be in another world. And there are the lies. I never know when to believe her about the children, and she lies to Daniel and me about each other.'

Louise still believes they can straighten her out, but wants me to know the situation. I feel like someone has kicked me in the stomach – I must have been blind not to see this coming.

The next few weeks were anxious ones, and I kept in close touch with Louise by telephone. She felt it best if I did not come over on weekends just then, since my presence might create a division of authority that would worsen the situation. Margaret continued to bring Jenny into the city for Sunday visits. The change in her demeanour was marked. She was tense and preoccupied, short-tempered with me and casual to the point of negligence with Jenny. It was painfully obvious that things could not go on as they were, but once more I could see no way to change the situation.

25 June 1967

An exhausting day. Went over to Wayne on the early bus to talk to Margaret. At first, her attitude towards me verged on the hostile. She accused me of being in league with Louise and Daniel to blame her for 'their own problems in their own house'. She calmed down a little as we talked, and finally admitted she has been drinking. Her excuse was 'I'm cooped up in this house all day long every day with all these kids, Mama. If I didn't drink, I'd go crazy!' That is understandable, I suppose. She has, after all, not yet turned nineteen, and it must be hard for such a young girl to be confined to the house so much. Silly me, I really believed our weekends together were enough to counteract that.

She is determined to leave Wayne, get a job, and live on her own. The very idea scares me to death, not only for Margaret, but for Jenny as well. If Margaret can't make it here, surrounded by a family who have nothing but love and concern for her, I am fearful she will never be able to establish and maintain her own home. In the end, I tried to persuade her to bring Jenny over to New York and stay with me, but she wouldn't budge. Will she ever find a happy life, I wonder? If she doesn't begin to change, what will happen to her? I'm not sure she knows how much I love her and want to help her. I'll just have to do the best I can to get that across to her and hope for the best.

Elizabeth noticed the change in Margaret right away. She had, from early childhood, been protective of her little sister, so when Margaret rang to tell her she was not going to stay in Wayne, I wasn't surprised that Elizabeth's immediate response was a caring one. On 1 July she and Kurt drove to Wayne and took Margaret and Jenny back to live with them in Madison Township, New Jersey. 'I am at home all day, Mama, and if Margaret wants to go to work,' Elizabeth told me, 'I can take care of Jenny at home. Don't worry about the expense. Kurt has been promoted to manager of the travel agency, with a much higher salary.'

Elizabeth's second child was due in September. I didn't think she needed two small children to look after just then, but she and Kurt were optimistic, and I had nothing better to offer. Hope flickered faintly that the two sisters could work things out.

3 July 1967
Margaret has a night-time waitress job in a roadhouse not far away from Madison Township. Elizabeth is upset because it is known for its rough and ready clientele, and rumour has it that drugs are sold openly in the bar. Margaret is delighted with herself. Elizabeth is willing to give it a trial period, but she hasn't much hope that it will work out for Margaret. Neither have I.

Within weeks, our worse fears were realized. Margaret was staying out all night, coming home drunk, sleeping all day until it was time for her to go back to work, and ignoring little Jenny. Elizabeth thought she was also on drugs. Margaret loved her new routine. Any attempt to get her to look for other work met with a defensiveness that defied opposition. Elizabeth's son, Lorenz, was born in early September, and Margaret's presence was more and more destructive to their family. Elizabeth worried, too, about the effect on two year-old Jenny of her mother's neglect.

Things finally came to a head. In response to a telephone call from Kurt, I left work and took a midday bus out to New Jersey. Elizabeth and Kurt had awakened Margaret to tell her that she would have to move out, and she was in a foul mood when I arrived. After listening to her go on and on about 'everybody telling me what to do', I lost patience and told her that, like it or not, she and Jenny had no choice but to come to live with me in New York. To my astonishment, she broke into tears and threw her arms around me, sobbing that she was so happy she would be going 'home' with me. Her need to be with me went straight to my heart. In spite of the tiny space in which we would have to live, my spirits lifted at the thought of having her close to me again.

In September 1967 I accepted a position as executive assistant to Allan Roberts, a brilliant financier who managed the investments of a New York millionaire family. His offices were in Manhattan, which eliminated the daily subway commute from Manhattan to the hospital in the Bronx and meant I was home about a half-hour earlier each day.

15 October 1967 2 a.m.

Margaret is finally in bed and – I hope – asleep, after prowling around the flat all night like a nervous cat. She begins work tomorrow as a night-time sales clerk at Alexanders [a large New York City department store]. The store is open until 10 p.m. every day, and she will work from six to ten o'clock five days a week. The pay isn't all that much, but at least the hours will allow her to take care of Jenny until I come home from the office.

It will be good not to have to listen to her rave on incessantly about her sister not showing her any respect at all as an adult and the wonderful job she had to give up. I've managed to say nothing and just listen tonight. She is also driving me mad in little ways that are probably petty on my part, but they really get under my skin. She will not stay in the room with the television or radio on, or else turns them so low it's impossible to listen in comfort. This from a girl who has always loved music and dancing. And during the day, she keeps the flat in almost total darkness, closing the drapes no matter how bright it is outside – I miss the sunlight.

I know she needs time to settle into all the changes, but it is hard to treat her with the respect she so much wants when she is so difficult. On the other hand, she is sometimes so loving and so anxious to please that it's hard to believe this is the same girl. This continual up-and-down of emotions is beginning to really get to me.

Despite the minor annoyances and as cramped for space as we were, things did seem to go well for the first few weeks. Margaret liked the hubbub of the large, busy store and was making friends with the other girls in her department. Once or twice, she joined them for drinks after work, but she was home within two hours after Alexanders closed. I was cautiously optimistic that she was coping with her drinking problem. I clung to the knowledge that alcoholics can, after all, reform, and she came home most nights in such high spirits it was easy to believe that she could be satisfied with social drinking.

I welcomed, too, the renewed closeness between us as she talked constantly of how much she loved me and Jenny and how grateful she was to be living with me again. Still, those protestations were so unnaturally intense that a sense of unease set in as their frequency increased. She is just reacting to an environment in which she felt safe, I told myself, indulging my own need for a sense of security. For the moment I was happy enough to forget just how adept Margaret had always been at misleading and manipulating those around her.

Gradually, her after-work drinking became more and more prolonged. She started to come home at two or three in the morning, obviously drunk, always gushing long monologues on how happy she was and how much she loved me for 'allowing me to be my own person'. It wasn't until a young girl in her twenties showed up at the flat after Margaret had gone to work and left a small envelope filled with tablets for her that I discovered her high spirits and much proclaimed love for me were directly drug-induced. When she insisted the tablets were only 'headache tablets' I simply did not have the moral courage to confiscate them, and I never found out exactly what those drugs were. But I realized then that there had been warning signals I should have recognized. Her make-up had become increasingly heavy and she took to showing up for work in outfits that bordered on the bizarre.

Worst of all, she was again neglecting Jenny. She refused to get up for breakfast with Jenny and me and slept all day, 'forgetting' to give Jenny lunch and getting dressed only at the last minute before she had to go to work.

How could I have missed those signals?

17 December 1967
Maybe there is hope for Margaret after all. Tonight she went to her first Alcoholics Anonymous meeting and came home full of enthusiasm for sobriety. A first. At long last she is admitting that she has a problem and wants to do something about it. AA has done such wonderful work with so many thousands of alcoholics, surely they will be able to help her. What a wonderful Christmas present that would be!

Margaret responded as much to the social contacts at AA meetings as she did to their programme of rehabilitation. As far as I could tell, she did stop drinking. One-half of her problems, I thought. If she could conquer drinking, then maybe she could break loose from the hold drugs had on her.

It was, however, at an AA meeting that she met James. A hardened alcoholic almost ten years older than she, he had for years followed brief periods of sobriety with week-long binges, inevitably followed by a return to AA and another spell of sobriety. By March 1968, she and Jenny had gone to live with him in the small upstate New York town of Dobbs Ferry, near enough to New York City for him to commute to work in Manhattan.

I felt ground down. It was obvious that nothing but trouble could come of Margaret's headstrong decision. No matter how hard I tried, she seemed hell bent on her own destruction. My efforts to head off that destruction were useless.

Futility took over.

One Sad Ungathered Rose

23 April 1968

Margaret called this morning. She and Jenny are in New York for the day. Later, she called to see if she and Jenny could spend the night with me. I was so pleased at the prospect. After work, met Margaret and took Jenny home so Margaret could meet James. Such a nice evening. Jenny was entranced by all the pictures and pans and copper moulds on the wall. Loved her bath in 'Granny's tub'.

Poor baby. She got homesick for 'my home' at bedtime. Almost three years old, this is the first time she has ever felt she has a real home, and I think she worries about it. To my relief, Margaret was home by midnight.

24 April 1968

Decided to stay home from work to be with Margaret and Jenny. So glad I did. Margaret looks so well, and seems so much more womanly than ever before. She seems to have found in James a strength and depth of feeling she's never known before, and she is responding in kind. Her concerns now are for basic values, not the shadowy, shallow things she has always known. Jenny is of real concern to her, and she wants to be sure to guide her through this period of adjustment. I think she is also struggling with a strong feeling of guilt, but James is helping her to see that is false. Margaret cooked dinner here in my apartment, and James joined us for a very enjoyable evening. Jenny was very relieved to see him, and as soon as supper was over, she was anxious to go to 'my home'.

A lovely, warm, family day.

A great weight lifted from my spirits after those two happy days. The doubts that had plagued me during recent months were lulled into silence.

The warm glow of family closeness was to last a short two days.

26 April 1968

Margaret called to see if I would come up to Dobbs Ferry Saturday when James comes home from work and stay through Sunday. They are having Betty Daniels from the Mahapac Clinic for the day, and she is a bit anxious about entertaining with James for the first time. She thinks I would help smooth things along, and it is nice for me to be needed. Later, she called back to say that James will be working overnight Saturday, so I'll go another time.

I'm really glad that things have happened this way, since it gives me a reason not to be with anyone Saturday or Sunday (Michael doesn't know plans have changed, so we hadn't made any plans). How I need a weekend for myself! My soul needs restoring, with a lot of privacy and a chance to do some of the things there is never time for.

That privacy was shattered on Saturday afternoon when James came to my flat to confide that things were not as they seemed. He was *not* working overnight. It had been Margaret's decision to cancel my visit. She had been drinking heavily during the day when he was at work, and James had talked her into meeting Betty Daniels, who ran a 'drying out' clinic in an upstate town that he had used many times. Betty was coming for the day to see first hand if Margaret's drinking warranted a stay in the clinic. Margaret had wanted me there initially, but then had panicked at the thought of letting me know about her drinking.

I was stunned. This was such a drastic reversal of the complete reassurance of the time Margaret had spent with me only two days before that it was difficult for my mind to cope.

James made a good case for her staying at the clinic and told me that he could arrange for day care for Jenny until her mother came home. I was far from confident that this would be a good arrangement, and I wondered about the effect on Jenny of staying with strangers all day. On the other hand, if Margaret was away only a short time, as James thought would be the case, it might be better for Jenny to stay in the home she had come to love. He left me with a heavy heart and once more completely at sea as to how I could help Margaret.

Margaret entered the clinic the next week, and although their rules prohibited me from contacting her by phone, I did speak to James each night over the next two weeks. He declined my invitations to bring Jenny in for weekend visits and obviously resented any suggestion that I come to Dobbs Ferry to see her. It seemed to me I was being shut out of her little life, and I have never understood James' reasons for keeping me away during that period.

15 May 1968

What a day! Just before lunch, James rang me at the office to say that he can no longer take care of Jenny and I would have to come and get her. His voice was so slurred that I know he is back on the drink.

I thank providence that I work for such an understanding boss. He told me to leave immediately and to take as many days as necessary to sort things out. One thing I know – this time I am not going to shift my responsibilities to Elizabeth or anyone else. Surely I can manage to take care of that precious little girl until Margaret is recovered and can work out some sort of future for the two of them, with or without James. I can't help but be a little anxious. After all, it has been almost twenty years since I took care of a child as young as Jenny, and I will have to dredge up all the child-care routines that have gone right out of my head after all that time. But I am very sure that this is the right thing to do, one way to help Margaret and do whatever I can to put Jenny's mind at ease about her mother.

Tomorrow I'll look into a nursery school or some other day care that will let me keep my job intact during this interim period. There are private day nurseries in this neighbourhood, but they cost an arm and a leg, and I simply cannot afford such fees. But there must be city-run centres for low-income parents – the trick will be to find one.

Jenny is such a sweet, trusting child. She has had so much

disruption in her short little life – I hope and pray I can bring
her through this safely.

Any other time, I would have been cheered by the train ride
through beautiful, warm May weather and a landscape bursting
with spring greenness, in dramatic contrast to the city's network
of concrete streets and highrise buildings. But with my
emotions in such a whirl, I hardly noticed my surroundings.

From the Dobbs Ferry train station, a taxi took me to
Margaret's flat, where I was confronted by the pathetic sight of
a staggering James trying to get cornflakes and milk together
for Jenny's breakfast, even though it was well past noon. She
climbed down from her chair and ran to cling to me as I took
over from James and gave her the cereal. The fridge held only
bottled beer, and I could not even find bread to make toast.

James called me into the living room and said I should
'hurry and get her out of here'. A neighbour had reported child
neglect to the social services agency in the town, and a worker
was coming that very afternoon to investigate. In light of the
disorderly apartment, James' dishevelled appearance and his
slurred speech, there could be no question but that Jenny
would be taken into foster care post haste. I simply could not
let that happen. Suppose Jenny grew up believing that her
mother had never loved her and had given her away, or worse,
that she herself were somehow responsible for her mother's
illness? On the other hand, there had been a strong bond
between Jenny and I since I had first set eyes on her. Maybe
staying with me would not be ideal, but I could not bear the
thought of my granddaughter going to live with strangers.

Jenny was content to come away with me on an early
afternoon train to the city. I knew that, not yet three years old,
she was bound to be bewildered by all that was happening to
her, so we talked about her mother being away because she was
sick. When Margaret was well again, I told her, she could go
'home' again. The sad thing, looking back, is that I truly
believed that.

Two days of exhausting telephone calls finally led me to Prescott House, a day nursery run by New York City, just a few blocks south of my street. Their fees varied according to the parents' income, and as Jenny's quasi guardian, I qualified for an incredibly low figure. The staff impressed me tremendously with their handling of emotional problems, as well as the physical welfare of the children, most of whom came from broken homes.

Those first few days had a decidedly comical aspect. As with all small children, Jenny didn't come complete with guidebook. With almost a twenty-year lapse since my last stint of looking after a small child, it was no easy matter to remember the strategies mothers use to help such a young one learn what to do and not do. I have never been at my best early in the morning, and now in addition to getting myself up and running, I had to deliver Jenny to Prescott House before going to work. However, the two of us bumbled along until we finally developed a routine that met her needs as well as my own.

In an amazingly short time, Jenny managed to settle in. As for me, it was wonderful to see the world again through the eyes of a child and find a delight in simple things that helped balance the worry about Margaret that had dominated my mind for so long. Our daily walk to and from Prescott House gave me a fresh look at New York streets as she found such pleasure in shop windows and street scenes I had never noticed. All in all, she seemed quite happy. So it came as a surprise when she asked if she could call me 'Mommy' instead of 'Granny' because all the other children had mothers to collect them. In the first of what she came to call our 'conversations', we sat down and talked it over. She did have a real mother, I told her, and even though Margaret was sick, she would get well, and then Jenny would want to call *her* Mommy. Did she really want to give that name to anyone else? I asked. She thought about it, then decided that it was all right, and even a bit special, to have a Granny take care of her for a while. Our first potential crisis was over.

Chapter Four

17 June 1968

Dear Mama,

I want you to know how much I appreciate your wonderful letter. It helped pull me out of a fog. You couldn't have said more of the right things. As for me, I'm fine. I start work again tomorrow, and I guess it'll be good for me.

There is a lot I should say, but I can't seem to find the words, and I've got more thinking to do. I hope soon I'll be able to write a long, long letter about all the things I feel.

Please let me know all about Jenny. What she is doing, etc. Does she still have pony tails? I love her very much.

Thank you again for that wonderful letter. Don't worry about me – James takes very good care of me.

Love,

Margaret

Margaret was released from the Mahapac clinic about a week before this letter was written in response to one I had mailed in time for it to be waiting for her when she returned to Dobbs Ferry. As I recall, my letter simply reiterated my love for her and my hopes for a happy future for her and Jenny. Her reply touched me deeply.

James was back in a period of sobriety and was convinced that Margaret had conquered her drinking. I agreed with him that it would be a mistake for me to be there with Jenny to welcome her home – the transition was bound to be difficult, and she would need time to find her feet and to know that she could stay sober on her own. Margaret had found part-time work as a waitress, and this was obviously not the time for Jenny to rejoin her.

Jenny was happily settled into her routine at Prescott House while I was at work during the day. I hesitated to tell her that her mother was home from the clinic, but that she couldn't go home just yet. Would she understand? Would she perhaps resent me for not taking her back to Dobbs Ferry? Perhaps resent Margaret for not coming for her?

With my own daughters, I had always felt very strongly that if I did not talk to them openly about our problems, the truth would surface sooner or later and cause more damage between us than facing the situation squarely at the outset. I decided to follow that same policy with Jenny. To my relief, she accepted what I told her without question. Only once in our years together did I deviate from that practice, and I will never forget the look of shock on her face when she discovered that I had kept things from her. Her only comment now was, 'Granny, will you come with me when Mommy is well?'

19 June 1968

Walking to work this morning, I chose the Second Avenue route solely for the one block from Second Avenue over to Third at 41st Street. The loading platform of The Daily News gives off such a warming smell of hot lead and ink, and passing it always makes me feel I've made contact with the wonderful world of print. Reminds me of my newspaper father.

I felt so good about the world I was moving through that when I turned the corner into 41st Street and that delicious newspaper smell met me head on, a smile automatically formed. There is something so nice about plain working men performing the physical work of loading the delivery trucks. About halfway down the block, from back in the darker recesses of the platform I was hailed by one of the men with 'Good morning'. It took a second greeting from him for me to realize he was calling to me. Such a friendly wave and smile – I guess he felt good about the morning, too.

I waved back and called 'Good morning' to him and walked on to my closed-in work day with the kind of glow that comes only from the reaching out of one person to another, even when they're strangers.

It was a simple incident, but one that lifted my spirits and, for a moment, banished the cloud of uncertainty that dulled my life so much of the time just then.

16 July 1986

Margaret is back in the Mahapac clinic, and tonight I feel such despair. James tells me that she has been picked up by the police twice for public drunkenness since coming home. They have, so far, brought her home each time, but who knows how many times they will do that. I am so very glad I didn't take Jenny back up there to live with her. I know alcoholism is one of the most difficult illnesses to overcome, but I also know that it can be done. But I am beginning to wonder if Margaret, after returning to such heavy drinking in spite of professional help, will ever be able to stay sober. James thinks she may also have been taking what he calls 'social drugs' – I don't know exactly what that term means, but my heart shrivels at the thought of her taking any drugs at all. James isn't sure about it, and I can only hope he's wrong.

Again, I had to tell Jenny that her mother was ill and that it would be a bit longer before she could see her. This time, I was far from sure that Margaret would be able to take care of her daughter any time soon, but I was able to talk about it without directly answering Jenny's inevitable 'when?'. She accepted without question my reply 'As soon as Mommy is really well'.

11 August 1968

The worst day of my life. Betty Daniels called to tell me that Margaret has broken into the medical cabinet at the clinic and is 'on dope'. She needs hospital care, Betty told me, and she stressed the urgency of my coming to take Margaret away as soon as possible. When I rang Elizabeth, she immediately left her children with Kurt and came into the city to drive me upstate. Mary Bellington [my next-door neighbour] offered to keep Jenny, who was delighted – they have become really good friends, and today Mary was a lifesaver.

While waiting for Elizabeth, I rang Dr Cherkasky to ask if we could bring Margaret to the hospital at which he works. Probably a real imposition – it has been a long time since I worked for him, and he certainly doesn't owe me any favours. That didn't seem to matter at all, and he contacted Irving Gottsegen [assistant director of the hospital], who arranged to keep Margaret overnight, even though they do not usually admit drug or alcohol addicts. Those two men will never know just how much their compassion and understanding have meant to me today.

When we reached the clinic, for the first time we learned that Margaret had attempted suicide through an overdose of drugs. I was so terribly shaken to see her in that condition. She was very dirty, make-up on at least a week, face broken out, feet filthy, lips swollen and cracked, one eyelid drooped even when she came around a little. When she opened her eyes there was utter loathing when she saw me – not only for me, but for herself as well. Agonizing trip back, with Margaret drifting in and out of consciousness on the back seat. Flat tire on

Parkway. Wonderful man changed it for us, saying 'I only ask that you help someone else'.

Such difficulty getting her admitted at the hospital. Thought for a few minutes I was going to have to ring Dr Cherkasky at home, but they finally located Mr Gottsegen's instruction to admit her. 'That trip could have killed her,' a young Emergency Room intern told me. 'She should have never been moved except by ambulance.' Talk about guilt – he really laid it on me. Elizabeth and I home about 10 p.m. Exhausted. Too tired to feel guilt or anything else.

Tonight my heart is heavy at the thought of what she must have gone through to reach that state. I've never loved her so much or felt so completely helpless. I don't know where she will go tomorrow, and my brain simply can't cope with it now – I am just grateful for my oldest daughter and good friends like Dr Cherkasky and Mr Gottsegen.

It had been a day of horror, and it was a relief to write it all down. I had spent the day trying to put on a cool, in-charge face and do whatever had to be done at the moment. There was no need to be strong in the pages of my journal.

12 August 1968

All day at the hospital. Can't begin to express warmth of my reception in Dr Cherkasky's office. Margaret was finally transferred to a larger hospital. I nearly reached my breaking point when the doctor there talked of releasing her in a few days. Pretty grim place, but at least she is safe.

An ambulance took Margaret and I downtown to one of the largest city-run hospitals in Manhattan. This was my first encounter with the misery of those who live in the blackest part of New York's heart. There was no shock there at Margaret's dreadful physical condition; it was as familiar to them as it was alien to me. We were kept waiting for more than an hour, Margaret still barely conscious on a stretcher, in a hallway crowded with others awaiting treatment for the entire spectrum of human ills – everything from internal aches and pains to knife or gun wounds. It was easy to spot the drug addicts, none of whom appeared to be as urgently in need of attention as Margaret. It was a severe test of my patience to wait silently when everything in me wanted to scream out to the over-worked interns and nurses as they scurried up and down the corridor.

When our turn finally came, I trailed along as Margaret was wheeled into a curtained-off cubicle. Another half-hour passed before a young intern bustled in, took a cursory look at her, instructed the nurse to give her an injection of some sort and to transfer her to a ward. He turned to leave, and I tugged at his sleeve to ask what was going to happen to my daughter. He was already immersed in a medical report for his next patient, and the poor overworked man was a bit impatient as he dragged the focus of his attention back to me. 'We will get her system free of drugs,' he told me, 'but we can't keep her here any longer than possibly three or four days.'

Every step of the way beside the stretcher that transported Margaret to a ten-room ward was a step through panic. There was no way that she could be fully recovered in three or four days. I knew it with a frightening certainty. What then? She was in no condition to go back to the fragile Dobbs Ferry set-up with James, and I shuddered at the thought of Jenny seeing her mother like this if Margaret came to us. Somehow, I would have to find more help to bring her back to health.

18 August 1968

Elizabeth drove in from New Jersey, and we went together to see Margaret. Her eyes are clearer than when I saw her on Wednesday, but she is still terribly ill. No hint of her being discharged soon, but I am holding my breath. Dr Cherkasky thinks she might be accepted at a state hospital, which has an alcohol and drugs unit, and he will set up an appointment for her and ask the hospital in which she is currently based to keep her until I can make arrangements for the transfer. Jenny went back to New Jersey with Elizabeth to stay for a few days.

Chapter Four

Dinner tonight with Michael at Parioli [one of our favourite Manhattan restaurants], then to an upstairs bar on West 28th Street to see the Greek dancers. That hypnotic music so moved me that without even being conscious of it, I rose from the table and danced to 'Zorba' music in the aisle on our side of the dining room. Somehow, that sound went straight into my very bones and in a strange way eased the pain of Margaret's plight.

22 August 1968

Rented a car and drove Margaret out to her next destination. My first time behind the wheel since Birmingham, and I am proud of myself for driving in New York for the first time!

I was really impressed with grounds of the state hospital and the competence of the doctors we saw. Dr Marterelli and staff did an exhaustive evaluation, but in the end would not keep her because her basic problem now is not alcohol. They cannot keep her in that district for psychiatric care.

What a shock! It never occurred to me that Margaret's problems could be psychiatric. So peculiar to hear her referred to as a 'mental patient'. What now? What kind of psychiatric problem? Is it possible their assessment is wrong? How do I go about getting help for her? How much longer will the second hospital keep her?

Margaret hardly spoke on the long drive out to the state hospital and at times slumped down in her seat, exhausted. She was still a pitiful sight, although she was at least clean and her face was devoid of the make-up that always seemed to herald emotional troubles. The hospital was a complex of red brick buildings on a large, wooded site that reminded me of a college campus. My hopes rose as we drove through the gates and past groups of strolling patients, some accompanied by nurses or male attendants. The pleasantness of the setting alone should, I thought, help in Margaret's recovery; certainly it was more conducive to good health than the seething chaos of the hospital in which she was based at present.

Margaret took no notice of the scene through which we

drove, and did not respond to my encouraging comments. The hostility I had seen in her eyes in previous days had disappeared, replaced by a blank, unseeing expression.

Dr Marterelli, a kindly, very professional man, saw us immediately, and a nurse took Margaret away for evaluation by senior staff members who would make an official assessment. As I waited on a bench outside in bright sunshine, I could not suppress the rising hope that this would be the place that would make her well again, that would restore her spirit as well as her body.

Some two hours later, I was called back in to see Dr Marterelli, this time without Margaret. They had done a thorough assessment, he told me, and all the doctors agreed that Margaret's problem was not alcohol or drugs, but psychiatric. They did not have the proper staff to make a definitive diagnosis, and their facilities are not suitable for mental patients. They have concluded that she is definitely psychotic, and they feel it is imperative that she get psychiatric treatment as soon possible. In the meantime, he promised to ring Metropolitan and request that they keep her as a bed patient until proper care could be found. He walked me to the door and I shall never forget his kindness as he put his arm around my shoulders and comforted me with the words 'Now don't you worry too much. Things will work out once she has treatment'.

On the interminable drive back to the city, I was grateful for Margaret's silence. I tried to look at her through different eyes and see the mental patient the doctors said she was. It had been such a struggle to accept alcohol and drugs, but this was different. Could anyone really cure mental illness? Was the rest of her life to be no more than a repetition of these past few years? Could they at least rid her of the drinking and dope? I was at a dead loss for answers, and I didn't know where to begin to look.

In late August *New York Magazine* bought an article I had written about Coney Island. It was my first attempt to sell my writing, and I was jubilant that a national magazine had accepted it. After the shock of Margaret's assessment, this personal achievement meant much more than it would have had my life been calm and serene. Even more importantly, it reaffirmed my determination to free myself from the nine-to-five world of business and make my living with words – any kind of words.

26 August 1968

What are you – you nebulous thing off there just out of sight, waiting to change everything for me?

This day has wiped away my elation of the Coney Island article sale. It was hard to concentrate on my work in the office as an inner frustration grew stronger every hour. I have such a sense of marking time, with an overwhelming feeling that some unforeseeable and unguessed-at happening will change all the circumstances of my life. Is it because Margaret is still in hospital and I haven't a clue what the future holds for her? Not entirely, I'm pretty sure – this feeling is about my life. Maybe it has to do with Jenny and our future together – am I deluding myself that she is with me only temporarily? I just don't know, but there is a certainty about these emotions that I cannot dismiss.

Never before with such intensity had I experienced what can only be described as a purely intuitive feeling. I struggled through the day, and just before leaving to collect Jenny at Prescott House, I rang Dr Cherkasky in sheer desperation. He was on the point of leaving for an important meeting, but put me through to Irving Gottsegen, who promised to contact the hospital the next day and look into psychiatric care for Margaret. I fell into bed that night still troubled about what lay ahead for me, never mind Margaret.

28 August 1968

Learned today that Margaret has appointment Friday morning (30 August) at the Clinic. All Irving Gottsegen's doing. The man is a saint! I know I have no real claim on him or Dr Cherkasky, but I honestly don't know what I would do right now without their practical help. Hope the hospital will accept her. One of best psychiatric hospitals in the country. She sounded so tense and worried when she rang to tell me about the appointment. Wanted me to go with her. I'll call the psychiatrist she will be seeing, a Dr Smythe, tomorrow to be sure he won't mind my coming. So glad Margaret wanted me along.

Dr Smythe turned out to be a woman in her early thirties. I could come with Margaret, she said, but I could not be present during her assessment. Her manner was curt on the phone, and so different from Dr Marterelli's that fear rose in my throat. From the sound of her voice, there would be little compassion for my daughter or for me from this doctor – she would find it easy to refuse admission for Margaret.

This hospital is, indeed, one of the best psychiatric centres in the United States. Many celebrities had undergone treatment there, and I knew the cost must be astronomical. At this point, that seemed a trivial worry. Somehow, I would find the money to cover *whatever* it cost. If they could restore Margaret's health, I would be willing to spend the rest of my life paying off borrowed money.

As Margaret and I travelled by taxi across town, I sought comfort in the thought that she might be heading towards a resolution of her troubles. At the very least, they would be able to determine if her problems really *were* psychiatric. At best, they were in a position to administer the treatment she needed.

30 August 1968

The monster that has stalked me the past few days has surfaced at last. Its name is schizophrenia.

Margaret is schizophrenic.That was the blunt verdict of Dr Smythe, delivered in a very busy public corridor where I had waited through her assessment. The diagnosis alone was enough to chill my heart, but it was made much worse by that doctor's cold demeanour – how could she be in that field of work and be so insensitive? She almost accused me of having caused Margaret's condition – as if I haven't felt that myself for years now. She will arrange for Margaret's transfer from Metropolitan by ambulance tomorrow, and her 'No, you can not come with her' pretty much shut me out of my daughter's treatment. When I tried to ask about the prospects for Margaret's recovery and if she would be able at some point to take care of Jenny, she was impatient, almost irritated. 'Even you should know that I cannot possibly tell you that at this point,' she said. 'It remains to be seen.' Cold comfort that! She might as well as added 'Idiot!' Silly of me to ask, I suppose, but I am left in such limbo I really needed to ask.

I don't even know what schizophrenia is. Years ago, I know everybody thought it meant a split personality and I know that disorder is now called multiple personality syndrome. It would have meant the world to talk to that doctor for even fifteen minutes and get some idea of what this illness is. Fat chance! I know she must be a very good psychiatrist, else she would not be on the staff at Payne Whitney, but I dread the thought of leaving Margaret in her hands.

Chapter Five

15 September 1968

Jenny and I finally were allowed to visit Margaret this afternoon. It has been a long fifteen days, and Jenny was beginning to worry that her mother 'is going to stay in the hospital forever'. Children are not permitted on patient floors, but Margaret was brought downstairs to a small meeting room so that Jenny could be with us. I don't know what to think about Margaret's condition – she is at least clean – the nightgown and dressing robe we sent her gave her a neat look, and that godawful makeup is gone. She looks much better than when I last saw her. But tonight my mind just isn't at rest about her.

She keeps telling me over and over that there is nothing wrong with her except drinking and drugs and that she can deal with them without being in the hospital. Hope flickers that she may be right. She has been off both alcohol and drugs for a long spell now, and at first she seemed almost like her old, sweet self. But her mood changed dramatically in the half-hour that Jenny and I could stay with her. Gradually that awful look of loathing crept back into her eyes each time she looked at me, chilling me to the very bone. What terrible thing have I done to her that she should feel such hatred? By the time we left, she was bitterly blaming me for keeping her 'locked up' and completely ignoring Jenny. Makes you wonder.

Truth to tell, I don't know just how Dr Smythe can separate the evils of alcohol and drugs from the schizophrenia Margaret is supposed to suffer – if I only knew more about the disease, maybe I could understand. No hope of that from Dr Smythe, but I know one thing for certain – tomorrow I am going to the Strand [a large bookshop with discount prices] and see if there are any books about schizophrenia that will explain it in language I can understand. Jenny kept asking me 'what's wrong with Mommy?' right up to bedtime tonight, and I don't really have an answer that will reassure her. I can only pray she won't grow up blaming me for sending her mother to a psychiatric hospital.

The next day Jenny and I spent almost two hours browsing through the stacks of new and second-hand books at The Strand. Jenny was incredibly patient and well behaved for a three year-old. In fact, the longer she stayed with me, the more I was coming to realize what an extraordinary little girl she was. The years ahead of us were to prove that time and time again.

My search turned up one or two medical texts that dealt with schizophrenia in such technical terms they were no help at all. In the end, I bought a book published in 1955. I had no idea just how outdated it was with regard to treatment, but it was written in such a style that I could understand most of the text. At that point I simply wanted to know about the illness itself. *The Human Brain*, by Dr John Pfeiffer, explained that the psychotic patient is sicker than the neurotic, since he or she is the victim of major mental disease. It went on to state that many 'mental' diseases are not essentially brain disease, but the result of disorders arising in remote parts of the body, disorders which biochemists and other investigators are learning more and more about. That statement alone was worth the price of the book. It cleared up for me the meaning of 'psychotic', a term that was rapidly becoming a part of my life. Writing things down has always helped me simplify complex matters, and after reading and re-reading most of this book, I once more resorted to putting into my own words the limited understanding it had given me.

20 September 1968

As best I can understand from this book, neurotics react to stress by bending their personalities and attitudes to meet it on their own terms. They are often difficult or obnoxious to live with, but are far from being mentally ill. Their problems are really psychological.

Chronic schizophrenics may react to stress in quite another manner. They may create a totally unreal world around themselves at one time, yet see reality with perfect clarity soon after. Just as a broken leg impairs the movement of the body, so a broken or distorted or weakened pathway to the brain, or an inadequate or oversupply of a vital chemical can impair the movement of the mind. When this happens, psychosis takes over the mind. Victims of such a psychosis may find that they hear voices where they see no bodies; see shapes where there are none; or feel they are being attacked by horrible creatures. Or, their minds may just go blank.

Increasing knowledge of the chemistry of the brain enables psychiatrists to use drugs to combat chemical imbalances that plague the psychotic. When stress becomes so great that the body reacts by an over- or under-stimulation of the chemical that controls emotional arousal, anti-psychotic drugs can counteract the disastrous effects. One drug will block out parts of the brain which react to the over-abundant stimulant, while another will synthesize that same stimulant when the body fails to supply it. This means that psychiatry can reduce the intense suffering of psychotic schizophrenics and virtually eliminate the danger they pose to themselves and those around them.

A million questions remained, but it was a start. If these 1955 definitions were still valid, then Margaret's problems seemed to me to be more neurotic than psychotic. The 'behaviour problems' of her younger years, for example, surely fell into the 'difficult or obnoxious to live with' category, and just as surely, alcohol and drugs might well be solely responsible for her most recent behaviour. Certainly I had seen no signs of her hearing voices or having hallucinations. Maybe the doctors were wrong after all. Still, she had many times manipulated me and her sister by presenting a distorted view of a situation, only to swing back to a clear, sharp version of reality just seconds later.

I was still deep in the throes of denial. Desperately needing to avoid the fact that my youngest daughter was mentally ill, I clung to the notion that for Margaret the answer was a matter of finding the right medication and helping her to avoid drinking and drugs.

If only the solution had proved to be that simple. That 1955 book made no mention of the schizophrenic's insistence that there is nothing mentally wrong, nor did it warn me of the cunning manipulation on which the schizophrenic mind thrives, or its inability to establish a stable home environment without outside help. All that lay ahead in a long, tortuous process of recognizing and acknowledging those symptoms for myself.

25 September 1968

My brain is in a whirl tonight, and I think this is the most frightened I've been since Margaret's troubles began. The administrative office at the hospital rang me at the office this afternoon to say that I must come in to see them and arrange payment by September 30 for Margaret's first month's treatment. The cost is just over $5000, and they must have it all by that date. I know that isn't really such a large sum, but my finances are already strained to the limit. 'It simply is not possible to spread the payments over an extended period, and you will be required to pay all charges at the end of each month', a Miss Butler informed me in a rather frosty tone.

Utter panic set in, and it was all I could do to keep going until five o'clock.

What am I going to do? It is almost impossible for a single woman to get a bank loan. I simply cannot ask Michael, and there is no one else in my life to whom I can go for the money. Besides, who knows how long Margaret will have to stay in hospital. Will they put her out if I don't come up with the money? And where will she get help if that happens? Will she come back to live with Jenny and I? With so much hatred in her heart for me, that is probably the worst thing that could happen to her.

I have never in my entire life felt so alone and so helpless.

26 September, 1968

Some saint above must be looking after me! I didn't sleep a wink last night, and this morning I was so preoccupied that Mr Roberts [the man for whom I worked as executive secretary and office manager] called me into his office to ask what was wrong. He has been so good about the times I have had to be away from work that I hesitated to tell him about the hospital bill. In spite of myself, tears came when I told him how impossible it seemed to find a way to pay the hospital. To my utter disbelief, that kind man waived a dismissive hand, asked exactly how much money was needed, picked up the telephone and instructed the Accounting Department to issue a cheque in that amount. I was absolutely dizzy with relief! I must have sounded idiotic in my gushing attempts to thank him and to assure him I would repay this life-saving loan. 'This is not a loan,' he said. 'Consider it an advance on the bonus you are entitled to at the end of the year. Now, go ring the hospital and see if you can take care of this today – we'll manage without you this afternoon.' Who else but a saint could have sent me to work for such a compassionate man!

When I took the cheque to the hospital around three o'clock in the afternoon, Miss Butler turned out to be a most understanding and sympathetic woman. I was able to explain my financial situation, as well as my fears for Margaret's continued treatment, candidly and without embarrassment. She listened attentively, and asked me if I had given any thought to applying to Social Services for financial help.

I hadn't – but if I had, I would have dismissed the thought instantly. True, it would be a way out of this mess right now, and she said all the paperwork for the application could be handled from her office. But when I agreed that she should go ahead with the application, my personal pride and sense of independence were a large lump to swallow. First time in my life I've had to look for welfare, and I don't know whether to be ashamed or relieved. She thinks she can have a disability allowance for Margaret approved quickly and if she does, I won't be billed any more – another blessing in this blessed day. Even so, I could cry at the prospect of my daughter becoming a charity case.

My mind is exhausted from trying to sort out just how I feel about today's developments. But, at least I'll be able to sleep.

Allan Roberts was a tough, demanding boss. When he was in the office, he expected me to work long hours beyond the normal work day, which meant that I often had to make hasty arrangements for Jenny to be collected from Prescott House no later than 6 p.m. and be looked after until I got home.

More than once I had debated looking for work somewhere else. Yet, all through this terrible crisis, he came to my rescue. Although I did, in the end, leave to accept a job that allowed me more flexibility in taking care of Jenny, it was with his blessing and a deep sense of gratitude on my part.

When I awoke the next morning, my feelings of shame and dependence on others had lost much of their power, although both would return to plague me from time to time in the years ahead.

17 December 1968

This morning, a telephone call from the hospital saying Margaret will be leaving tomorrow brought on a numbing attack of pure panic. She will be coming here to live with Jenny and me, and I am scared to death. Suppose I say or do something that will set her off again. Nothing I have been able to find in print makes any mention of how schizophrenics should be treated at home. After fretting about it for hours, I rang Dr Smythe and asked to see her before I bring Margaret home. She agreed to an appointment only a half-hour before Margaret would be discharged – seems like a frighteningly short time to be really helpful, and I can only hope that she will be a little friendlier to me than she was when Margaret was admitted.

It turned out to be a rotten day. My talk with Dr Smythe lasted all of fifteen minutes, most of which were filled with a severe rebuke that I would dare ask her to violate 'patient confidentiality', my first encounter with a term I would come to detest. Because the Pfeiffer book had stressed the importance of medication, I asked for instructions in seeing that Margaret took whatever medication was prescribed for her. Again, Dr Smythe replied with a dismissive 'Margaret knows all about that – you don't have to concern yourself with it'. How often in the future I was to remember that statement with amazement and disbelief!

My spirits hit rock bottom as I waited for Margaret. At least, I thought it was rock bottom. But they sank even lower when she finally came through the patients' door, looked at me with naked distaste, and announced defiantly that she had no intention of coming home with me. She was to meet James at five o'clock at his workplace and go back to Dobbs Ferry with him. Not one word about Jenny. With dead certainty that this was inviting disaster, I held my tongue and gave her taxi money and the few extra dollars I could afford.

To be honest, a great wave of relief swept over me, calming the turmoil that had filled my mind since the day before. There was, after all, nothing I could do.

Nearly three months later, when I next heard from Margaret, it was to learn that she was once more hospitalized. As 1969 wore on, a distinct pattern emerged – three months in hospital followed by about three months of being on her own, then another three months commitment in yet another hospital. My own life took on an unreal quality as I struggled to juggle hospital visits, Jenny's wellbeing, and office responsibilities. Sleepless nights were filled with searing anxieties and a myriad of questions for which I could find no answers. There was so much I did not know about schizophrenia. What, I wondered over and over, was going on in Margaret's mind to cause such confusion and pain. And why, with the same home environment, had this terrible affliction attacked her and not Elizabeth? Occasional newspaper or news magazine articles gave glowing accounts of the 'deinstitutionalization' of schizophrenics and other mental patients, praising drugs like Thorazine, Mellaril, Trilafon, Compazine, and Stelazine that made such a programme possible. Lumped together under the umbrella name neuroleptics, they reduced the thinking disorders that underlay the psychotic phase of schizophrenia. Why were they failing Margaret? Had the doctors simply not yet found the wonder drug that would work for her? On every hospital visit, I requested an appointment with her doctors in a desperate attempt to understand. Amazingly, not one hospital found it convenient to arrange such a meeting. My feeling of isolation was devastating.

Between psychotic breaks Margaret lived with James in Dobbs Ferry, periodically left him to stay with Jenny and me, and then disappeared for weeks on end. Through it all, she vehemently denied that she had any mental problems and invariably failed to continue her medication. Her sudden appearance at my apartment late at night, dirty and distraught, tearfully protesting her great love for me, became a regular occurrence, as did her sudden disappearances. To this day, I have no idea where and how she lived during those absences.

Each hospitalization came when there had been no contact between Margaret and I for several weeks, and when she had been missing for a long period, each time the telephone rang I half expected to hear an impersonal voice tell me she was once more in hospital. Years later, when Jenny and I flew to Austin, it was clear that Margaret's memory had twisted events of that time. With all the force of a physical blow, she was to hurl at me the accusation 'I could never understand, Mama, why you kept putting me away in all those hospitals'.

Disruption was taking over my life, exacting a terrible toll. I struggled to reconcile the self-evident state of Margaret's progressively worsening mental condition with the surge of hope accompanying each hospitalization that it would be the last, that some doctor would be able to make her well.

Michael and I grew closer that year. He was a great comfort and many times stayed with Jenny when I dropped everything to respond to one of Margaret's calls for help. True, he found it difficult to understand my eternal optimism in the face of what he saw as a hopeless situation. But, I told myself, he is not a mother, and I suppose most mothers hold on to hope when there really is none.

The constant swing of emotions and the never-ending search for just the right words to say to Jenny dominated my every waking hour and quite often invaded my dreams.

Chapter Six

In early January 1970 I accepted a position as office manager for Dr Richard Peters, a prominent ophthalmologist with offices just off Park Avenue. His was a busy practice, but with a staff of three, my hours were more flexible than in my previous job. It was a pleasant office, with congenial co-workers, and contact with Dr Peters' patients went a long way towards brightening my days.

22 February 1970

Early this afternoon I just couldn't stand the worry about Margaret any more, and for the first time since she has been sick, I rang the Missing Persons Bureau of the New York Police Department. She left the hospital two days ago to come home to Jenny and I, but never showed up. Certainly not the first time she's gone missing, but this time she had seemed happy at the thought of being with us. I have to keep pushing away visions of her lying dead somewhere in a Manhattan alleyway. And in spite of the hospital's discharging her, she didn't look all that well when I visited her last Wednesday. The police didn't hold out much hope and reminded me that she is twenty-two years old, legally an adult, not technically missing from my home. Cold comfort, that. And the officer with whom I spoke was so dismissive that I doubt he even wrote out a report – they must get hundreds of calls like this every day, and I guess they do the best they can.

Four days later Margaret called. She was back with James, but said she would be home at the weekend. The weekend came and went with no sign of her until early Monday morning when she appeared at our door. She was very dishevelled and nervous, prowling around the little apartment in the stiff, jerky movements I had come to recognize as side effects of medication after every hospital stay. I wondered if medication was also responsible for the unhealthy bloat of extra weight.

I decided to keep Jenny home from Prescott House and to take a day off from the office to be with the two of them. Always in the back of my mind was the thought that her daughter, now five years old, would eventually be able to break through to the real Margaret and bring about the miracle doctors could not accomplish. This time, however, Margaret was so preoccupied and restless that, even when I suggested things for the two of them to do together, Jenny stayed close to me, as though frightened of her mother's behaviour. As I began to prepare our dinner, Margaret suddenly walked out the door, saying she needed cigarettes, and she was gone again.

6 April 1970 3 a.m.

There are just no words to express my feelings tonight, and I would give the world to have someone – anyone – to talk to. Margaret is back with James and they have just called, obviously very drunk or strung out on drugs. They spouted such a harangue of abuse that I came close to hanging up the telephone, but finally managed to get them to slow down so I could grasp the sense of what they were saying. 'You took my baby away from me, Mama, and I'll never forgive you for that. And you're not getting away with it any longer.' The raw hatred that coloured those words literally left me in a cold sweat. Then James came on the telephone to say that they were leaving Dobbs Ferry right then on his motorcycle to come and collect Jenny and take her to live with them. 'You have no right to keep her', were his final words before they hung up.

I am sitting here now looking at Jenny, sleeping so peacefully, and I feel so helpless. To see her taken away by Margaret and James when they are in such a state would be the end of me. For so long I have yearned to see Margaret take responsibility for this wonderful child, but not like this! Still, I know that in the eyes of the law James is exactly right – I don't have any right to keep her with me, even when I know it is a matter of her physical safety. Dobbs Ferry is a pretty long drive in a car from Manhattan, probably longer on a motorcycle, so I have made a pot of coffee. All I can do is wait and hope I can talk them around to leaving Jenny here, at least for the time being.

It was an all-night vigil, and by dawn they still had not come. I dared not run the risk of taking Jenny to Prescott House, for fear they would take her from there. Instead, I told her we were taking a day off to buy her a new outfit, but that I had to see someone on business first. I rang Dr Peters' attorney, who agreed to see me before noon in view of the urgency in my voice, and Jenny and I were out of the apartment by ten o'clock.

The attorney told me that I would need an Order of Protection. He explained that this was a Family Court matter and I would not need legal representation, only enough documentation of Margaret's mental problems to demonstrate to a judge that she should not have custody of Jenny at this time. He arranged for me to appear in Family Court the next day and helped me decide which letters, hospital reports, and the like to take with me.

8 April 1970

FAMILY COURT OF THE STATE OF NEW YORK

CITY OF NEW YORK

Certificate of Order of Protection Issued

ORDERED AND DIRECTED, pursuant to Article 3 of the Family Court Act, that said parent shall observe the following conditions of behaviour, to wit:

Petitioner's, Susan Poole, custody of the above named child not to be disturbed; child not to be removed from school by respondent Mother.

AND IT IS PROVIDED BY LAW that the presentation of this Certificate to any Peace Officer shall constitute authority for said Peace Officer to take into custody the person charged with violating the terms of such Order of Protection and bring said person before this Court and otherwise, so far as lies within his power, to aid the Guardian, Susan Poole, in securing the protection such Order was intended to afford.

This Order of Protection shall be and remain in force until a further hearing ordered for 24 April 1970.

Elizabeth drove in from New Jersey early that morning to take Jenny home with her and I spent an exhausting day in Family Court. To see so much human distress in that waiting room, packed with children of all ages and their distraught parents trying to get them to sit down and be quiet would touch a heart of stone! Court clerks scurried in and out of the closed courtroom to and from the one small cubicle that served as their office, and I marvelled at their patience with parents who intercepted them time after time, demanding to know when their case would be heard.

The judge before whom I appeared must have heard versions of my story many times before, for it was a remarkably short hearing. His approval was for a Temporary Order of Protection. The hearing later in the month, he explained to me, was to give Margaret an opportunity to appear before the court and regain custody of Jenny if she chose to do so. The official Order was hurriedly typed up and signed, and I left the courthouse with a profound sense of relief, but with a heavy heart.

Elizabeth rang soon after I arrived home to say that she would keep Jenny a few days more. Jenny adored her aunt and two cousins, and I was once more grateful for such an understanding older daughter.

Jenny was, at least for now, safe and happy. But an irrational 'How could you do such a thing to your own daughter?' sat on my shoulder and all the logic in the world could not budge it. Guilt hung heavy in the very air, and it pulled me apart. Margaret was my child – my baby despite her adulthood. Surely I owed her every support and protection. Yet here I was resorting to a court order against her in order to protect Jenny, *her* child. It would be years before I would be able to fully accept the fact that protecting and nurturing Jenny was virtually the only gift I could give Margaret.

10 April 1970

Dear Margaret,

Just a note to let you know that you will be receiving notice of a hearing in Family Court here in Manhattan on Friday, April 24, to give me a temporary Order of Protection for Jenny. This seems to be the only practical thing to do just now, but I wanted you to know it before you receive the court's notice so you won't panic.

I love you very, very much.

Mama

12 April 1970

Dear Mama,

I love Jenny too much to take even a chance on hurting her any more. With you, she's got a chance. With me, I don't know.

I won't go to that hearing. I am not staying away because I love James, but because I love Jenny. Please keep me informed on how she is. I'll do the best thing and stay away from her.

I love you both very much.

Margaret

When I presented Margaret's letter to the Family Court on 24 April the judge postponed the hearing until 1 June and extended the Order of Protection until that date. I assumed Margaret was still in Dobbs Ferry with James, but when a notice arrived in the mail of her voluntary commitment to a state hospital on 10 May, although I was surprised, it did not come as a shock. In the years since her first hospitalization, I had seen Margaret wander in and out of institutions, manipulating one hospital staff member after another when it came to diagnosis and early release. I was beginning to develop a numbed scar over emotional shock, and it came as no surprise to me when a telephone call to the hospital revealed that Margaret had managed to convince them that her troubles were nothing more than alcoholism. Dr Marterelli, who had seen her two years earlier, was no longer there, and I resisted the temptation to remind them that they must have records of his diagnosis of mental illness. But resignation had begun to set in, and I simply decided to leave well enough alone. After all, she was in a safe, protected environment, and that seemed enough for the moment.

25 May 1970

Dear Mama,

Dr Dawson told me you had called. I can't for the life of me figure out how you found out I was here.

I received the notice to appear in court 1 June. If you would, I would appreciate it if you will explain to them where I am and ask them to postpone the hearing. I imagine that the hearing is about custody of Jenny. I'm very grateful that Jenny has you right now, and I will sign temporary custody papers if necessary. But under no circumstances will I sign any permanent custody papers. You know as well as I do that it isn't necessary. I have not bothered you, calling or coming around upsetting Jenny, and I never will. Please let me know if they will postpone the hearing and notify me as to the new date.

Thank you for writing. Please write again and let me know how Jenny is, what she feels about my leaving, etc. Someday, I'll be well enough to have her with me and do her no harm.

I have just about everything I need here except a robe. It's not too bad here, but very difficult to get out.

Love,
Margaret

4 June 1970

Dear Margaret,

Just a quick note to let you know that the hearing was re-set for 8 July, and I'm sure you will be receiving a notice from the court. If you shouldn't be able to attend, it will probably be put back again. Please don't be concerned about it – there is not and never has been any question about permanent custody.

I haven't answered your letter sooner because I just haven't known how to or what to do. I know so well how much you love Jenny and want to see her. On the other hand, she has been very deeply upset by this last separation and I'm not sure what more uncertainty and confusion would do to her.

Your doctor feels we should wait a while before letting her visit you, so you and I both will have to try to think of Jenny first and put our own feelings behind our concern for her.

I love you very, very much and want to do the things that will make you feel better and that will help you. But Jenny is such a precious little girl and has so much sensitivity that we have to be very careful to protect her as much as we can.

Do you want me to come out without her? I don't want to push you in any way and will wait to hear from you before planning a trip out.

All my love,
Mama

30 August 1970

Dear Mama,

It was good to see you Sunday. Thank you so much for coming.

I had good news this morning. I went in front of the staff and the doctor told me I could leave soon. The social worker will help me get a job and an apartment. I can't tell you how much better I feel. Don't worry, they won't let me go until I'm ready. If you have any connections that could help me with finding an apartment, please call the social worker out here. I feel so much better than I was feeling. It's wonderful to enjoy life again. It looks beautiful.

I love you very much,

Margaret

The Margaret I had known when she was young shone through this last letter. Suddenly, it seemed unimportant that there had been such a long silence between letters and that she had let two further postponements of the court hearing come and go with no word. And just as suddenly, I embraced the conviction that she was at long last free of whatever had so devastated her, be it alcoholism, drugs or schizophrenia. That conviction flew in the face of everything I had read about recovery from schizophrenia, but there seemed to be so many uncertainties in the medical profession about its diagnosis and causes that it was easy to believe Margaret had weathered a severe mental storm, even if schizophrenia were involved.

On 8 September, the court finally extended the Order of Protection until mid-November 1971. It was only a formality now, I told myself. With a job and a home of her own, surely Margaret would no longer be a threat to Jenny's safety. The temptation was great to tell the judge to forget the Order – that Margaret was well. However, the small inner voice of instinct that I had learned to trust over the years whispered that I should just let it be, so I said nothing.

I was riding a wave of euphoria as I hurried home to ring Margaret to let her know of this latest development, just in case she should receive a notification from the court and be upset about it.

That joyful wave came to a resounding crash when the hospital informed me she was no longer there. Margaret had been discharged the day after her last letter and had disappeared. The social worker had been unable to locate her to follow up with work and a place to live.

It was 23 November before we heard from Margaret when she rang at 1 a.m., and 9 December before she came home. By 20 December, she had gone again. Christmas Day was brightened for Jenny and me when Elizabeth and Kurt and their two children came in from New Jersey to have dinner with us. But Margaret's shadow hung over us, and I wondered just how and where she was spending this day that had always been so special for her.

Chapter Seven

My 1971 journal is a chronicle of unremitting disaster. Crisis followed crisis, and because most of the emergency calls were almost always in the early morning, I placed a copy of the Serenity Prayer, 'God grant me serenity to accept the things I cannot change, courage to change the things I can, and wisdom to know the difference' beside the telephone to help me hold at bay the panic that set in with every emergency.

Although Margaret returned to live with Jenny and me in January and once more tried to hold down a job at Alexanders, by the end of March, she was again deep into psychosis.

29 March 1971
Margaret very ill. Called police to keep her from leaving.

30 March 1971
Margaret to hospital. Dreadful day. Home 1:30 a.m.

For the first time, I found it impossible to confide in my journal my deep hurt and the painful confrontation with the truth of

Margaret's condition. I had been aware that her mental state was becoming more and more fragile over a period of days, but once more I had been unable to find a way to ward off the impending crisis. On 29 March when I came home from work, Margaret was in a semi-hysterical state and Jenny was frightened. Margaret insisted that suicide was her only way out of a world in which no one cared for her and that I was conspiring to keep her 'locked up in a loony bin', and to turn her daughter against her. There was no way, she said, that she would endure another hospital stay.

When she seemed determined to walk to the East River, only a few blocks away, and end all her pain, it scared the wits out of me, and as a last resort, I called the police to see if they could help me get medical help for her. It seemed hours before they responded, and I was in a state of panic as I followed her down the stairs from our sixth-floor flat, trying all the while to reassure her that I did love her and that she was safe living with me. We had actually reached the ground floor of the building before two young police officers appeared on the scene. Margaret's demeanour underwent the same dramatic change I had seen when she so skilfully manipulated medical people who were trying to assess her condition. In a convincing manner that bordered on flirting with the two young men, she told them that I was no more than a possessive mother trying to prevent her leaving home to be on her own. My heart sank when they told me that since they had only my word that she was suicidal, there was no way they could compel her to go into hospital. Treating the whole thing as a family row, they finally talked her into going back upstairs with me to reconsider her decision to leave.

I climbed those stairs with her in a daze of sheer relief struck through with recurring panic. My memory of that exhausting night is still dimmed by the overwhelming fear that kept me talking non-stop as Margaret's mood swung between stinging accusations and slobbering declarations of love for me. It wasn't until early evening of the next day that she began shaking violently, as though with a chill, confessed that she had been taking drugs for several days and that she had no more pills and was beginning to crash. 'Either get me a fix, Mama, or get me to a hospital,' she moaned. When we reached the city hospital in our district, they took one look at her, refused admittance, and sent us to another hospital for psychiatric treatment rather than a drug overdose.

In retrospect, I think my inability to write about the distressful experience of that night was rooted in the beginning of my abandonment of hope, a process that was to stretch over several years. Two days passed before, safe in the haven of my little flat, I found emotional release in the form of a short story that was published many years later in a leading Irish magazine, *Woman's Way*. Feelings I had not been able to express in my journal poured out through fictional voices.

Chapter Eight

19 May 1971

Dear Mama,

I want to apologize for the upset Sunday. Most of it is the medication. The doctor and social worker talked with me today, and I couldn't agree with them more. It's the three-year-old in me that keeps hanging on to you, and it's time that the twenty-three year-old takes over. I will stay here and learn to walk alone on my own, with their help. Thank you for being so kind Sunday.

You're a good mother. I just have to learn to live without you, and I know I can. I'm going to join a group tomorrow for people who have been on drugs and are trying to stay off. It's like group therapy. I think it will be good for me to get involved in something like that, since I have a problem with drugs.

Mama, thank you for helping me Sunday. Please forgive me. It won't happen again. Wish me luck, and try to write

when you can. I love you very much, and I know you love
me.

Love,
Margaret

In mid-April 1971, Margaret had been transferred from one
hospital to another. In the course of my visit on the Sunday
before the above letter was written, she had lashed out at me so
vehemently that attendants on her floor came to end our visit by
physically dragging her back to her locked ward. The only 'help'
I had been able to offer was to persuade them to leave her with
me, assuring them that she would do me no harm. I read through
Margaret's letter with mixed emotions. A creeping cynicism
dampened the hope of her eventual recovery that had been
renewed so many times in the past when she wrote in this vein.

22 May 1971

*Coming home from work on the subway this evening, my feet
slipped on a page from one of the daily newspapers that
someone had thrown on the floor. It was much trampled, torn
and creased, but I picked it up and, until my eye caught the
word 'schizophrenia' I planned to throw it in a litter basket
when I reached my station. I smoothed it out enough to see that
this was one of a series of articles the paper was running on
mental illness, and today's subject was schizophrenia, so I
folded it as best I could to take home.*

*Psychiatrists, the writer said, are divided into what he
called 'nature versus nurture' schools of thought as to the cause
of schizophrenia. If this theory is right, all Margaret's suffering
can be laid squarely in my lap, and after re-reading my last
letter from her, it is easy to believe it fits the two of us like a
glove. 'A clouding of the mind that springs from a poor home
environment dating back to early childhood', the article stated.
It even spoke of 'schizophrenogenic mothers', defined as
'schizophrenia-causing' mothers, and went on to suggest that
such mothers were dependent on their children's illness as the
core of their own lives and, either consciously or unconsciously,*

actually perpetuated the situation. This group believes that psychotherapy to change the mother as well as the schizophrenic is the only effective treatment. 'Continued on page 42' came right in the middle of a definition of nature as '. . . a biochemical or physiological imbalance of the. . .'

Sweet Jesus – could I be one of those horrible mothers? Could that account for Margaret's swings from love to hostility? She is obviously undergoing psychotherapy in the hospital, which probably means the doctors there feel there is some basis for thinking her illness is linked to me. Is it possible that what I believe is cynicism is really a subconscious resistance to her recovery? Can it be that I am dependent on all her calls for help in her never-ending crises? In my heart, I know that isn't true. What I want is to see her well and living a healthy, normal life so that I can be free to live my own. But the thought has left me shaken, and I wish now I had never picked up that blasted newspaper page.

By June Margaret's mental state was so little improved that my sense of hopelessness had grown deeper. Hope had long sustained me, and this blight of depression was taking a terrible toll, making it increasingly difficult for me to deal with everyday life.

In desperation, I made an appointment to see a psychiatrist about my own frame of mind. His counselling boiled down to the one practical step I rejected with every fibre of my being just then. 'Any family is only as strong as its weakest member. You are going to have to accept that and cut all ties with your daughter. There is nothing you can do for her; if she finds the help she needs, it will have to come from someone outside the family. For your own sake, you must focus on your own needs and those of the rest of your family.' I know now that wisdom lurked behind those words, but at the time it was shielded from my vision by a stubborn veil of love and obligation to my child that was part and parcel of my concept of motherhood. His words evoked the disquieting memory of that newspaper article, even though he in no way even hinted that I could have directly caused Margaret's illness.

1 October 1971

Margaret came to the office for the new coat I bought her, then went with me to pick up Jenny at Prescott House, and have dinner at Rocky Lee's [an inexpensive pizza restaurant]. She's not good at all – obviously hallucinating and talking to voices in her head. Jenny a little frightened, and she cried in the taxi going home. We left her school books in the taxi, which upset her even more. When the driver returned them about a half-hour after we got home, his kindness helped dilute the sadness that overwhelmed both of us.

For a time, things went smoothly when Margaret met Jenny and me for a light supper, and I could see Jenny beginning to relax in her mother's presence. Suddenly, it all went wrong, as Margaret became preoccupied, dropping out of the conversation, and slipping into an intense question and answer exchange with voices we could not hear. I hurriedly paid the bill and hustled Margaret and Jenny outside, where we put Margaret in a taxi to return to the hospital and then hailed one to take us home.

This first encounter with hallucination left me deeply shaken. 'Hearing voices inside her head is a part of Mommy's illness', I told Jenny. 'The doctors at the hospital are trying to make her better', I added, trying to reassure myself as well as this little girl who was trying to cope with such a huge monster of fear. Still, I could not disguise the anxieties that haunted my own heart, and from this point onward, I shared them with Jenny. She seemed to find some comfort in knowing that she was not alone in being afraid for Margaret. A terrible burden for such a small child, but I knew instinctively that if I were to shield her from all the things her imagination might conjure up, I would have to be open and honest about every development. God forbid that she ever feel that she was in any way responsible for what was happening to her mother! And I knew that was a real possibility if she did not know the truth.

Chapter Eight

Later that month, even though Margaret could hardly have improved greatly, she was discharged from hospital and vanished.

10 November 1971

Margaret rang me twice today to say she is in a downtown hospital and begging me to come get her out. Her voice is hardly recognizable, and the second time she called, someone there took the telephone from her in mid-sentence and hung up the receiver. Devastating.

Always in the past when this kind of call came, I had dropped everything, left my work, and rushed to give Margaret whatever help I could. This time, however, that instinct was dulled by the newspaper piece. The psychiatrist's words 'You are going to have to cut all ties with your daughter – accept that there is nothing you can do for her' also surfaced. In the end, I took the first small step towards acceptance. I decided to finish the day's work, collect Jenny at Prescott House, and go home instead of rushing to the hospital. Because my work was beginning to suffer from the interruptions of emergency dashes to my daughter's aid, I made it through another work day before going to the hospital in the early evening. A day-and-a-half of raw agony. Yet, I felt the stirrings of an inner strength for having taken that decision.

11 November 1971

After work, Jenny and I headed downtown to see Margaret. Couldn't see her. She set fire to the 4th floor and all patients had to be evacuated.

Sheer exhaustion prevented my putting into words the whirl of emotions that stayed with me through that terrible night. The first shock had come when a rude attendant sneered as he informed me, 'Oh, you can't see *her* – she's the schizo who set a fire and we had to move all the patients on that floor. She's put us all through the wringer, I can tell you.' Nor, he said, could I talk to any of the attending doctors on duty. 'They're much too busy getting all those patients settled. Come back tomorrow – you might be able to see her then.'

Two more days passed before I was allowed to see Margaret. My heart froze when I was led to a small, locked room and an attendant rose from the single chair in one corner to admit me. The room was bare except for a mattress on the floor and the attendant's chair. Margaret, dressed in a rough hospital gown, stared at me with open hostility and refused to respond when I spoke to her. When tears closed up my throat, I told the attendant I would have to leave, and huddled in a corner, Margaret watched me go through the door.

Composure had deserted me, and my legs were suddenly like rubber. I was in no state to go back downstairs where Jenny was waiting, so I leaned against the corridor wall, eventually stemmed the tears and regained some semblance of composure. Jenny, who by this time had adjusted to the fact of the fire, sat quietly while I told her that her mother was still very ill. I gave silent thanks to whatever powers there be that she had not seen Margaret in that cell-like room. 'Don't worry, Granny,' this little six year-old tried to comfort me, 'maybe *this* hospital will make her well.'

On the way home guilt set in and stayed with me through that long night. I had to wonder if, after all, I had done the wrong thing to delay my visit for so long. Would Margaret have set that fire if I had come immediately?

The next day, an intern at the hospital rang to tell me that immediately after I had left her, Margaret had picked up the attendant's chair and hit him over the head. Could I come in for a talk with the hospital's social worker, he wanted to know. Not before time, I refrained from replying. My request to see her doctor was turned down with no reason given, but the social worker agreed to see me after work the next day. My journal for 16 November records only the terse statement 'Not much hope that Margaret will get long-term help'. A month later, she was transferred back to a state hospital.

Chapter Eight

16 January 1972
Went to see Margaret at the state hospital. She had a day pass and came home with me from 2-7 pm. Jenny was glad to see her, but a little upset. I wonder if that's because of the way she looks, or Jenny's own uncertainty about Margaret's state of mind. She is still very sick, I think.

18 January 1972
Margaret released from hospital and moved to an Upper West Side welfare hotel. I am so fearful that she is not yet capable of managing on her own. If only someone could check that she takes the medication that keeps her on an even keel. Her resentment towards me, for whatever reason, makes it impossible for me even to mention medication to her.

The hotel to which Margaret had been sent was one of several SROs [single room occupancy] hotels in midtown and the Upper West Side of Manhattan used to house mental patients on the mend. They were a vital element in New York State Department of Mental Hygiene's 'deinstitutionalization' policy for emptying its psychiatric hospitals. Once thriving commercial or residential hotels, by the late 1960s and early 1970s they had deteriorated into near-slums, with callous, uncaring management. Rooms were dark, dirty, and littered with alcoholics and drug addicts who were also consigned to such quarters by the social welfare system. By the early 1970s, more than 10,000 mental patients were estimated to live in SROs – physical assault, rape and robbery were commonplace. Schizophrenics had little recourse in protecting themselves against personal crime. Even when they turned to the police, they often were not capable of explaining what had happened. In most cases, their reports are dismissed out of hand.

11 April 1972
Went to CBS administrative offices to hear tapes of their mental health series. They did shed a little light on schizophrenia, but not much that I didn't already know, and I

still feel so very ignorant. If I could only understand what goes on in Margaret's head, there might be a chance I could help her, or at least not do any damage.

During those first few months of 1972, Margaret made periodic visits to see Jenny and me. She seemed to be coping with her accommodation and was getting some outpatient care from the hospital. It was through their efforts that she was moved into an apartment, with the proviso that her attendance at the clinic would be regular rather than spasmodic.

On the first day of May, I held my breath and took one of the most important steps of my personal life – I resigned from my office job to embark on a freelance writer life. It was scary! At the age of forty-six, I had no savings and I had to face up to the fact that I probably never would be able to accumulate significant money in the bank. True, I had one or two prospects for writing assignments, courtesy of one of our patients, a non-fiction book editor who had seen some of my writing. My native optimism gave me the courage – or perhaps it was sheer nerve – to believe that, without the time and energy required for office work, eventually I would be able to make a living with words. In the meantime, I could fall back on temporary office work when necessary. For the next year-and-a-half, I 'temped' all over Manhattan, but finally landed on my feet with guidebook assignments for one of America's leading travel publishers. The pay was moderate enough, and it has been a continual juggling act to arrange travel and, at the same time, take care of my family responsibilities. But the books took me as far afield as New Zealand, Holland, Belgium, Luxembourg, Ireland, the south-eastern United States, and New Orleans, with life-enriching experiences all along the way.

6 May 1972

Moved second-hand furniture down to Margaret's new apartment, and Jenny and I took dinner in to her. God-awful part of NYC, on the Lower East Side in a building that looks to be inhabited with the lowest form of street life. I felt a sense of danger all around.

10 May 1972

I had a call this afternoon to say that Margaret didn't show up for her appointment at the hospital. They asked me to go downtown and check on her. When I got there, she was home and looked O.K., but was a little withdrawn. She says she will keep her appointments from now on. If only the mental health profession would recognize the fact that schizophrenia renders its victims incapable of managing their own treatment! Margaret simply cannot manage to put her outpatient appointments on top priority. At least the social worker did call me – a first, so maybe he will continue to follow up.

For the next few months, Margaret's demeanour swung between high good spirits and severe depression. When things were especially good, at my suggestion she took Jenny home for overnight visits, and once for a weekend. My faint hope that she would find normality through love for her daughter had long since died, and Jenny has since told me that those visits were very distressing to her as a seven year-old. From a logical standpoint, it was the wrong thing of me to do, and even from an emotional standpoint, I cannot think why I was willing to put Jenny in what could well have been a very dangerous situation.

23 July 1972

Lovely sunny day on 'tar beach' [a New York term for a flat rooftop often used for sunbathing by apartment dwellers]. May Kiely [a neighbour] was on the roof and I learned she has a little house in Ireland which she will sell me for $2,000. My own little corner of the world, at last! I know so little about that country beyond 'Wearing of the Green' and 'I'll Take You Home Again, Kathleen'. Lot of learning to do.

There was no way then for me to know just what a major turning point this would be in my life. Acting on pure instinct,

I arranged to borrow the $2,000 and began to read everything I could find on Ireland. On the surface, it did seem a foolish thing to do in the light of the deepening closeness between Michael and I. Still, I could see no clear signs that it would last far into the future. Michael seemed content to leave our relationship on a less-than-marriage basis, and the prospect of ending my productive years without a place in the world that belonged to me had haunted me for some time. Added to that was a budding conviction that there would be little or nothing that I would ever be able to do to help Margaret. It was becoming more and more clear to me that I would have to get on with my own life, allowing as little disruption from her as I could manage, and do the best I could to raise her daughter. So, all the negatives notwithstanding, I was delighted and began immediately setting aside a little of each pay cheque to finance a trip across the Atlantic to see my new home. A permanent move was certainly not in the immediate future, but there were years ahead of me in which to furnish it for my later years, with or without Michael.

MARGARET IN FULL HEALTH, 1981
Margaret during a brief interval of sound health in 1981 when she went to live with her sister Elizabeth in South Carolina. Just eight days after this photograph was taken she was once more in hospital in the throes of yet another psychotic break.

MARGARET AND HER MOTHER, AUGUST 1995
The day after our 1995 reunion in Austin the camera caught Margaret in one revealing moment when she dropped the artificially smiling face behind which she attempted to hide the ravages of her illness during the eight years she had been lost to us.

MARGARET AND JENNY, AUGUST 1995
The pathos of Margaret's reunion with Jenny in August 1995 is heartbreakingly clear as Margaret impulsively threw her arms around her daughter in a mixture of joy, regret and sadness for the illness that had robbed them of so many years they might have had together.

Chapter Nine

Today was such a warm, sunny day that Michael, Jenny and I took a long walk. When we sat for a few minutes in the sun on the steps of a Catholic church, Jenny was curious about the interior of the church, so I walked her inside. She was awed by the vastness, the rather overpowering altar, the stained-glass windows, the statues, and the candles flickering in their red glass holders. She pulled me down and whispered, 'What were all those people doing?' When I answered that they were saying a prayer, she wanted to know if we could say a prayer, too. So we entered a back pew, she bent her head, folded her hands, and whispered 'Please God, let it work out for me to live with Mommie'. Then, she looked up at me quizzically, and I whispered 'Amen', which she repeated, then told me 'I have another thing to say to God, Granny'. Bowing her head again, she added 'And God, please don't let Mommie ever get sick again. Amen again, God'.

Jenny's poignant plea to the Almighty was an arrow straight to my heart, and I knew that no matter how much love and attention I was able to give her, nothing could erase her longing to be with her mother.

10 March 1973

Jenny is staying with Margaret for a week as a trial for living with her permanently. To my complete surprise, I'm going through agonies I never expected. Her going was my suggestion, and a strong motivation (though perhaps not a very noble one) is my need for more time to myself. I've longed for the freedom and quiet times alone of those two years when I first came to live in New York. But, with the move made, I find myself unable to clear my mind of worries that Jenny will lose some of the values I've tried to develop in her. She's such an inquisitive, intelligent, responsive little creature, and it would be such an enormous waste if she moved now, at eight, into a haphazard, casual world where her questions are not fully explored and her sense of order is not respected.

I find it difficult not to call constantly to see if she brushed her teeth, got to bed on time, is in school on time, did the extra school assignments, etc., etc., etc. ad nauseam. The real basic care will be there, I'm pretty sure, but I'm not at all convinced that the more subtle necessities of her little soul will be recognized and nurtured by Margaret.

Margaret is yet another concern. This is the opportunity of her life so far to meet the responsibilities of being Jenny's mother and of learning the marvellous satisfaction to be had from fulfilling them. My heart aches for her in the tremendous effort she is making. More than anything else, I have to struggle against pressuring her so much about details that, instead of being the strength she needs to draw on, I turn into the very force that makes the transition impossible for her to make. God help me! I need a true guide through the next few days and weeks!

Once again, my heart had overruled my head. Logic told me

that as long as Margaret's personality was so volatile she simply was not capable of shouldering the responsibility I had foisted on her. Logic, however, had little effect when pitted against Jenny's heart-wrenching prayer.

I should have listened to logic. Only a few days after this journal entry, in the late afternoon, a panic-stricken Jenny rang me to say that Margaret had been sleeping all day and she could not wake her. When I rushed downtown to that grim little apartment, I found my daughter comatose, and unresponsive to all my efforts to bring her around. It was obvious that she needed medical treatment, and quickly, but when I rang her social worker at the hospital, I was met with the disdainful reply that 'Margaret knows who her friends are and that we are here to help her. If she needs us, she knows where to call'. Hurt at being cast in the role of an interfering mother, I rang the city's emergency ambulance and because Margaret was an outpatient, I was able to persuade them to take her to that hospital. She was admitted and remained an inpatient only briefly, before being transferred back to the state hospital, where she was kept under constant 'suicide watch'.

16 March 1973

Dear Mrs Bunyon:

I am sorry if I 'goofed' in calling you when Margaret was in crisis. As you say, she is an adult and does know where she can get help when she needs it. But it was very difficult to be objective about such things when she could not be roused and was not capable of calling on her friends for the help I knew she so very much needed.

There is, perhaps, no way in which I can really assure you that my call was not prompted by any lack of respect for Margaret's privacy or her right to seek whatever aid she felt she needed from whatever source she chose, but rather from a very real concern for her safety and the recognition (a very painful one) that because of her hostility towards me I cannot help her. But I do want you to know how much I appreciate all that you and the hospital have done for her. If there is ever anything I can do, please call me. Otherwise, I will leave the situation to Margaret and to you and hope that she will face and overcome any future regressions without lasting harm to herself or others.

Sincerely,
Susan Poole

I had been deeply hurt. And I was angry. Both those emotions would probably have remained unspoken but for my fear that this social worker's attitude towards me might adversely affect her treatment of Margaret. I seethed inside at the necessity of explaining *to a professional* my concerns for my daughter.

In mid-July, Margaret walked away from the state hospital and disappeared onto the streets of Manhattan. Two days later, when I learned that she was gone, a telephone call to the police revealed that no missing persons report had been filed by the hospital. There was nothing they could do without such a report, I was told, despite the fact that Margaret was in a dangerous mental state that made it vital that she be found as soon as possible. I finally reached a young patrolman who reassured me that he would instigate a search for her. Later that very night, when he was off-duty for the day, he rang to tell me she had been found in Washington Square, a notorious drug addict hangout, and had been admitted to a psyschiatric hospital. My gratitude for his kindness was so intense that I promptly wrote a letter of commendation to the New York Commissioner of Police, who replied and assured me that it would become a part of the patrolman's official record.

The hospital is one of New York's oldest psychiatric hospitals, widely perceived by the public as a sort of holding pen for mental patients and alcoholics during periods of crisis. I must confess that to a large extent I shared that perception, and when I visited Margaret there, it was reinforced by the grim appearance of the place and my memory of her brief stay there in 1971. This time, however, I met with compassionate understanding from two of her attending doctors who, over-worked as they were, sat down and explained much of just what was going on with Margaret.

'You must remember,' the older of the two said, 'that to schizophrenics, the way they act and the things they say make perfect sense. Their distorted senses and trains of thought make their actions seem entirely logical and rational. The only protection for those who care for the schizophrenic is to try to separate the illness from the person – not an easy thing to do.'

'No one will ever understand fully just what is in the mind of a schizophrenic at any given moment', the older man said, 'but we do know about some of the distortions that cause so much grief. For one thing, virtually every one of the physical senses is intensified. Patients have told me that all kinds of light, from bright sunlight to the glow of a television set, become unbearably intense. Their hearing plays tricks on them – I don't mean when they are hearing non-existent voices, but they have said that in a crowded room, all the sounds may be quite indistinct except for certain *specific* voices, or street sounds outside may bellow out so loudly that voices inside are drowned out. Even the sense of touch can be heightened to the point that just brushing against another person can bring on acute physical pain. We can alleviate those conditions and ward off psychotic breaks to some extent with medication, but I have to tell you that so far we have had little success in curing them permanently.'

It was the first light anyone had ever shed on some of the most puzzling aspects of Margaret's behaviour.

'As for paranoia and the inability of schizophrenics to function in everyday society, we are still searching for answers.'

'But what about the drinking and drugs?' I asked. 'Why is she so often seen simply as an alcoholic and a junkie?'

He looked at me sharply before replying. 'There are those who will tell you that most schizophrenia these days is drug induced – that treating the drug addiction will eliminate schizophrenia. In Margaret's case, that simply isn't true. Her history makes it absolutely clear that alcohol and drugs are *symptoms* of schizophrenia, not the cause.'

It was her hostility towards me, Elizabeth and sometimes Jenny that had brought me perhaps the most pain over the years. 'Well, you see,' he explained, 'that is one of Margaret's self-protection devices. She feels she is constantly misunderstood, which creates real pain and loneliness for her, as well as deep fear, that your misunderstanding is based on your hatred of her, which you are covering up by professing to love her. As unreasonable as it seems to the mentally well, she has worked out that for her, all love is only a mask for hatred, and there is danger in accepting or giving love.'

Could I do anything to get beyond that misguided reasoning, I wanted to know. Thoughtfully, he scanned through Margaret's medical history, then hesitated before replying. 'I must be candid with you,' his expression was one of genuine sorrow. 'Margaret's symptoms apparently occurred at an early age and, judging from her history, intensified over a relatively long period of time. With that kind of history, there is little or no probability of her complete recovery. That, I know, is practically impossible for you, as her mother, to accept.'

That word 'accept' sounded a warning bell in my head. 'Does acceptance mean that I can best help her by cutting all ties with her?'

'I don't really think so.' His voice was filled with compassion. 'If you can learn to see her illness for what it is, and if you can accept that it has little to do with you personally, you can also learn not to expect rational behaviour from her. You can be there for her when she is stable and see that she gets medical attention during psychotic breaks. Beyond that, I cannot tell you exactly how to deal with Margaret, but it may help you through the difficult times to know that, in my professional opinion, *you didn't cause her illness and you cannot cure it*. Most mental health professionals now take that view.'

What a massive blow to guilt! If I could manage to hang on

to those words, what a blessed relief it would be. No more agonizing over my past mistakes. And, I thought silently, if I could only accept at face value this doctor's bleak prognosis for Margaret's recovery and resist my native optimism, it would put an end to the emotional turmoil that regularly took me to the pinnacle of unrealistic hope only to cast me back down into the depths of utter despair.

Those two doctors, whose names I did not record in my journal, threw me a lifeline that day. I fully understood that their crucial word had been 'if', but it was a big 'if' and I have to this day been unable to accept completely that I have not been responsible in some way for what has happened to Margaret. Nevertheless, the veil of ignorance that had caused me so much anguish was partially lifted, and as I left the hospital, I felt stronger and better able to cope with whatever lay ahead for my precious daughter who had suffered so much.

That strength was sorely tested when I went to see Margaret the next day. Dressed in a shapeless grey hospital gown, with unkempt hair and a sullen expression, she seemed to be in a semi-zombie state. Without a word, she handed me a scribbled note, then turned and walked away.

> Mama, I don't know why you're doing all this. But I pray you stop. I couldn't have hurt you enough to make you want to hurt me so much. All this pain is so unnecessary. Please stop. Love, Margaret.

Shattering. As though someone had given me a hard punch in the stomach. No matter that the doctors had told me I was not the cause of her illness, it was obvious that *Margaret* held me responsible. With all my heart, I wanted to break through that wall of hostility and blame to hold her, to cradle her in my arms and comfort her, to shield her from such pain. I wanted to help her see the world through eyes of delight again, as she once had seen it.

By the time I had left the building, tears were streaming down my cheeks and I found it impossible to walk on trembling legs. Leaning against the iron railings that surround the hospital, I stood sobbing aloud, crying for a jumble of reasons – for Margaret, for myself, and for little Jenny. Crying has never been an easy emotional outlet for me, and this is the only time I can remember weeping in public. When the tears finally stopped, I was drained, and it was all I could do to board a bus to go home.

Later that year, the following letter from my father overflowed with concern and comfort. How sad, I thought, that no matter how hard I tried, Margaret was unable to accept the heart-warming love that my father's letter expressed for me, and which I so wanted to give her.

7 May 1973

Dear daughter,

I've been constantly thinking about Margaret's condition, and worrying too about what effect it might have on Jenny. I know it's a terrible burden on you – any mother worries a lot when her children are having problems, especially when there is so little she can do to really help the situation. There's little I can say that would be much consolation. But, having had a few occasions when we worried about our children, the best advice I can give is to pray a lot, do the best you can and leave the rest to God and the child.

You said on the telephone last night that Jenny is to spend the summer with Elizabeth and Kurt, that they are fixing up a room for her, and that they plan to set up a college bank account for Jenny along with their children. Kurt also mentioned to you the possibility of trying to get guardianship of Jenny.

Now, I've been thinking . . . wouldn't Jenny really be better off living with Elizabeth and her family all the time? She would certainly receive love and affection along with good care, and would also be living with other children and not altogether in a grown-up world. She would have someone to play with, not only at school, but at home, and that means a lot to a child. And, though I know you would miss her like a front tooth, it would relieve your burden somewhat and not keep you tied down as much. Can't help but think it would be best for all concerned, and I do feel it's worth giving serious consideration and thought.

Love,
Daddy

It was as though my father had reached across the miles and wrapped me – and even more importantly, Jenny – in a warm embrace of loving concern. I rang him immediately and promised to give a lot of thought to his suggestion. I also had to tell him that the prospect of being permanently separated from Jenny was more painful than I would have ever expected. Anyway, it wasn't a decision I had to make just then.

When Jenny left to spend the summer with her cousins, Michael and I decided to make our first visit to Ireland to see the little house I had so impulsively bought up on my rooftop. As I walked from the plane at Shannon Airport there was a strong, near-spiritual feeling of being where I was meant to be. In the two weeks we were there, that feeling grew into an illogical certainty that Ireland must some day be my home, no matter how far in the future that might be.

To say that I lost my heart completely to the land itself and even more so to the people we met is an understatement. The very landscape had for me the look of eternity, as though its mountains, rivers and lakes had been there since the beginning of time and would remain until time comes to an end. There was a great sense of security and safety in that landscape for me that had nothing whatsoever to do with logic.

As for the people with whom we came into contact, there was a genuine warmth as they welcomed us to bed-and-breakfast homes, and a real interest in seeing that we enjoyed our stay. The soft sound of Irish voices invariably had an underlay of humour, and for the first time, I was keenly aware of how scarce that commodity has become in America. Even more important to me was the sheer kindness of everyone we met, their concerns not only for us, as visitors, but for their own neighbours; their quick, verbal compassion for their own countrymen who might be in trouble. Then, there was their view of life as circular, a recognition that life and death are part of the same coin (obituaries very often stated 'died after a short illness, but in the fullness of time'). It had been a *long* time since I had encountered that sort of attitude in my home country. Even back then, I was not so naive as to believe that Ireland was without its scoundrels, but somehow the panache with which they practiced their blackguardism lessened its impact.

In the years since, my love for Ireland and the Irish has grown steadily. Perhaps the most meaningful blessings of my live came when I was finally able to make Ireland my permanent home.

At the end of the summer, Elizabeth and Kurt wanted Jenny to stay on with them at least over the winter school term. Despite all the logic of my father's letter, I had put that possibility out of my mind and had not really given it serious thought. That little girl had become so much a part of my life that logic faded when confronted by my selfish desire to keep her with me. Funny – I would gladly have seen her go to live with Margaret if there were any realistic hope that she would be safe. Yet I had qualms about sending her off to live with what I knew to be a loving and safe family. Still, I had to recognize the benefits of the life she would have with Elizabeth and Kurt that I simply could not provide, so in the end I agreed.

By October 1973, Margaret had been transferred to two different hospitals, and finally released to yet another welfare hotel.

10 October 1973
Hospital waiting room 10:30 p.m. to midnight. Confusion of emotions. Helplessness followed by resentment. Strong thought, 'she's twisted – flawed in some way I don't understand. I won't give up my life for one that's twisted!'

Chapter Nine

A terse journal entry was all I could manage after a horrifying few hours. A hysterical Margaret had appeared at my door hurling at me one accusation and obscenity after the other. 'You bitch, you can just turn off that machine you have in the middle room!' she shouted. 'I know you've been giving me dope and poisoning the air in the hallways to make me sick. I'm on to you, and I know damned well Mollie [our Scotch terrier] is in it with you!' She was in such a state that I could not be sure what she might do. Frantically, I reminded myself that it was Margaret's *illness* we were witnessing, not her true self, and from somewhere came the strength to remain calm. I ignored her outbursts, made a pot of coffee, and eventually was able to quieten her down. It took nearly an hour and several cups of coffee for her to reach a halfway rational point, and to my surprise, she meekly agreed to let me take her to a hospital emergency room. My heart was in my throat as we went by taxi back to the hospital, then waited until midnight for her to be admitted.

11 October 1973
*Saw Father Dolan re Margaret. Not much help. Maybe I just
don't have real faith. Since I found the Ethical Culture Society,
I have not felt any deep need for it. Thought I might find solace
just now from a more religion-orientated organization, but it
certainly wasn't there today.*

It is a measure of my need for understanding and compassion – for myself as well as for my daughter – that I went to see a Catholic priest in the neighbourhood church. The poor man did the best he could, I suppose, but in my distressed state he seemed indifferent to the depth of my pain, and in the end he could only suggest that he would pray for us both, which was of little comfort. In retrospect, I think it was a search for *human* rather than divine compassion that sent me to Father Dolan.

Religion was a significant part of my growing-up years, and Methodist Church youth activities had been important to me. As adulthood wore on, however, organized religion of any denomination became less and less meaningful. Eventually, it was the man-made rules and regulations of all churches that drove a wedge between me and religious institutions. From a spiritual standpoint, I have always been far more moved by the wonders of the natural world and the innate goodness of most people than ever I have been within formal religion. I have never felt a need to put a name on whatever divinity from which those things spring, and I am quite happy to leave the designation of a Christian God, Mohammed, or some other divinity to those for whom they do meet a very deep need. I do not count myself an atheist, but rather an agnostic. I *do* count such mysteries as life after death as treasures of our 'this world' existence. Death, it seems to me, is life's last great adventure, and I am content to keep an open mind, without holding on to any hard and fast faith.

For some time before she left, Jenny and I had been going across town to Ethical Culture Society Sunday School for her and lecture services for me. The Society's only creed was 'Man's ethical behaviour to man', which seems to me to embody all the moral teachings of the major religions. Ethics are, after all, based on respect and love, and I firmly believe that if one adheres to *ethical* behaviour, all the other details will take care of themselves. Jenny, in the meantime, was learning about *all* the major religions in Sunday School, which would provide a good foundation for making her own informed choice when the time came.

Chapter Ten

20 January 1975

Manny Fleischman [a drug dealer living and operating out of a Manhattan hotel] telephoned during the afternoon to say Margaret was in crisis. I dropped everything at the office and rushed up to West 102nd Street to see her. She was in a very bad way after keeping Manny awake most of last night, alternately screaming 'Help' and 'There's a corpse in the bed', then hiding under the bed, refusing to come out.

She was relatively calm when I got there, but the wildness was lurking in her eyes, and she couldn't speak without breaking into tears. 'Stripey', the little stuffed dog that Jenny had sent her was first hugged tightly, then ignored, than grabbed up again. When I left, she seemed to be drifting off to sleep, so if the fates are good, she will sleep through the night and be much better tomorrow.

Sometimes I have to wonder if whatever God there is cares, or even knows, about those sufferers like my Margaret.

Only a few days before this call, Manny had phoned to tell me that Margaret had been living in an uptown west side welfare hotel during the weeks I had not known where she was, but was now staying with him.

Manny Fleischman was one of the more unsavoury men with whom Margaret found refuge. A huge bear of a man, he lived in a sleazy uptown hotel. I never learned how or where the two of them had met, but by the time he let me know that Margaret was with him, my first reaction was relief. I had learned to turn a blind eye to the shady characters who wandered in and out of her life.

Because of his size, Manny was also the first to inspire fear – fear for myself as well as for Margaret. In spite of that, and even though the very sight of the unkempt, unshaven Manny turned my stomach, there was the hope that Margaret would have regular meals and a roof over her head, at least for a little while.

When his call came, that hope died. I knew in my heart that she was on the verge of another psychotic break. All the signs were there – the heavy make-up, dirty clothing, and eye expressions that swung from wildness to blankness.

21 January 1975

Another call tonight from Manny to tell me that while he walked me to the subway last night, Margaret had taken over 40 tranquillizers, and he just didn't know what to do with her. I didn't have the nerve to ask him where she got that many pills, and when I asked about her condition tonight, he just said, 'You'll see when you get here'.

All the way downtown on the EE subway train to West 42nd Street and then on the Broadway Local subway up to West 103rd, there was such a feeling of dread in my heart. I couldn't believe that anything too dreadful had happened to her – I didn't have that instinctive sense of total despair I've had so often in the past. Yet I knew it was possible – maybe even probable – that I would find her dead. It was that old, familiar uncertainty – the worst part of this whole thing.

Chapter Ten

It was a long subway ride, and all sorts of things went through my mind – what I'd have to do if she were dead; how I'd get through the ordeal of handling details like calling the police; how I'd manage to keep my composure enough to take care of things; whether I'd have to feel guilty at being relieved for her that her torment was ended; whether this would be, instead, another long night of getting her to the hospital for another hospital session.

I thought that ride would never end, and yet I almost wanted to stay on the train and never get off. When I finally reached Manny's hotel, I found Margaret dressed and really quite calm. Manny had cooked a pot of chicken stew, and they acted as though this were a social visit, with Mama coming over for supper!

My reaction was so quick I almost couldn't handle it. After that long, anxious subway ride, finding her like this triggered a blinding rush of anger, followed by an immediate wave of relief. Maybe it was just that I was so tired from working all day under the cloud of worry about her. Maybe I felt abused that Manny hadn't told me on the phone that she was all right.

I feel such helplessness. She's headed for another psychotic break, I'm certain, and I don't know of anything that can prevent it or that can help when it comes. We've been through it so many times already, and I truly don't know how she'll be able to endure that kind of agony again.

If Manny has the endurance – he seems to have the affection – to see her through the next few days, maybe she'll begin to come back without reaching that breaking point. There's just no way to know.

30 January 1975

Manny called to say he couldn't take it any more and had sent Margaret back to her hotel. 'I've given her uppers and downers right out of my stock – she's costing me money and she gets loonier and loonier,' he said. 'I got plenty of customers for them pills, and I ain't charging her nothing.' He's a drug dealer, for God's sake! He hasn't the faintest notion that the drugs he's

107

feeding her actually cause her psychosis – what a different story it would be if someone could see that she took the medication that would help as regularly as she seems to gravitate to those peddled by Manny!

When I remember the lovely – truly lovely – person being destroyed, my whole insides turn to tears. God, is there no way to keep this terrible waste from happening?

I hurried to Margaret's hotel to be sure she was all right. If Manny's hotel was sleazy, this one was far worse. Not only was it dirty and dimly lit, but it was peopled with obvious dope addicts, some of whom looked quite dangerous. My reception at Margaret's shabby little room was a surly 'Go away, Mama, and leave me alone'. She never let me beyond the threshold of that room, and I left with no clear idea of her condition.

3 February 1975

The call from a large city hospital up in the Columbia University area did not really come as a surprise – I've halfway expected it since Manny's call. I rushed right up, and found Margaret in a distressful physical condition, obviously from too many and too different a mix of drugs. She was barely conscious when I saw her and kept dozing off, so I didn't stay very long.

8 February 1975

When I went up to the hospital to see Margaret this afternoon, a doctor on her ward told me she has been released this morning and has returned to her hotel. I went into a real panic. When I saw her last night, it is true her physical symptoms were very nearly gone, but it was painfully clear that her state of mind is far from stable.

Late in the afternoon, when I arrived at the hotel, she wasn't there and hadn't checked in. So, once more, she is on her own. Is she wandering the streets? Did she go back to Manny? A great sense of futility fills my heart tonight, and I can only pray she will get in touch with me soon. I will call

*Manny tomorrow – just can't cope with it tonight – but I doubt
if he will take her back again.*

It was the beginning of another long stretch of not knowing
where and how Margaret was living. No matter how many
times she went missing, my worry about her during those times
never seemed to lessen.

I still did not know Margaret's whereabouts in March when
my mother called from North Carolina to say that my father,
now seventy-five, was in a critical condition. I flew down immediately, putting concern for Margaret to the back of my mind.
He had been ill for several years, first with heart problems, then
lung cancer, so the call was not entirely unexpected. Both my
parents had been staunchly supportive and forthcoming with
practical help when I needed it, and the loss of either would be
devastating.

13 March 1975
*Daddy died today. So glad I have been able to be here with
Mother these few days and to spend some time with him. I
don't know if he ever understood the depth of his children's love
for him and our appreciation of all he has given us.*

My parents had always been such a solid unit in the minds and
hearts of their three girls that it was difficult for us to think of
one without the other. Actually, as his brothers and sister
gathered for my father's funeral, there was such deep love and
appreciation in the memories told and retold in the family
group that he was almost a palpable presence. It seemed
impossible that he was gone. Mother, of course, felt his absence
more keenly than any of us, and I decided to stay with her as
long as possible to help with those first difficult days after the
rest of the family left.

22 March 1975
*Today is Margaret's twenty-seventh birthday. Where is she?
How is she?*

No matter that my mind was preoccupied with the loss of my father and concern for my mother – Margaret always hovered in the background.

I returned to New York on 29 March, sad to leave Mother, but relieved to be back in my own little refuge, all the funeral hubbub behind me.

29 March 1975

Waiting for me in the accumulated mail was a note from a non-denominational home in Garrison, New York run by Christian individuals and financed by private endowments. Margaret enrolled herself there on 28 March. The note said that residents must stay for one year and can have one visitor one Sunday a month. I won't try to visit her tomorrow, but will try to go the first Sunday of next month. When I rang, the call was put through to someone in the Administrative Office who told me Margaret was recommended by another mental patient she had met during one of her hospitalizations. Wouldn't it be wonderful if religion turned out to be the very thing to pull her back to normality! Even if she turns into one of those fanatic Christians who go to such extremes in their beliefs, it would be so much better than the life she has been leading.

23 April 1975

Margaret left the home today. The person who telephoned to let me know said they have no idea where she was going. She simply walked out. How long will it be this time before I find her?

It was to be almost two months before I was to hear from Margaret again. In the meantime, payment for my writing assignments was so slow in coming that I went to work for a few weeks as a temporary secretary at McGraw Hill, one of the largest publishers of educational books in the United States. The Friday pay cheque was regular and made it possible for me to keep up with current expenses. The work also gave me an insight into the publishing business that would prove invaluable over the next few years.

It was during one of my McGraw Hill assignments that I came across a book they had published the year before on mental illness, with the off-putting title *Madness and the Brain*. Browsing through its pages, I was excited to discover that its author, Dr Solomon H. Snyder, wrote in a conversational tone that made complex matters easier to understand, and that the bulk of the book was devoted to schizophrenia. I hurried home to read that enlightening text, and I was to return to it time and again in the future.

For me, this book unravelled many of the illness' mysteries that had most troubled me. I learned that Margaret's hostility to me and other members of her family probably stemmed from the fact that 'schizophrenics are so weighed down by overriding and intolerable emotions that to stay alive they must hide their feelings from the world and, as far as is possible from themselves'. In a chapter headed 'Making Sense of the Schizo-phrenic Mind' another paragraph had a special meaning for me: 'He may shield himself from the perceptual onslaught and block out from emotional awareness the impact of his environment, especially the impact of the truly important people in his life. Thus, even at an early state, he will turn off the world and turn his maladaptive perceptual antennae inward. In this way, he will become preoccupied with his own internal fantasies which, though somewhat unpredictable, are certainly more under his control than the capricious external world'. Elsewhere, Dr Snyder explains the fears that beset the schizophrenic: 'The world is for him a frightening, very dangerous place . . . When given a traffic ticket, he feels he has been labelled a murderer. If Mother shouts at him, he fears she will kill him.'

Much of the book expanded and reinforced the advice to recognize that Margaret's behaviour could not be expected to be 'normal'. I resolved to be there for Margaret when she was stable and to get medical attention for her when she was in crisis.

Chapter Eleven

2 June 1975

JENNY CAME HOME! So glad to have her back. Elizabeth and Barbara [Elizabeth's close friend] drove her home from Philadelphia, where they have been visiting Barbara. I have missed Jenny terribly, and no matter what the future holds for both of us, I just know it is better if we face it together. Even though she is not usually a demonstrative little girl, she has stayed very close to me all day and seems especially happy to be back.

When I asked her if she still planned to be an ice skater, she replied that she still wants to learn to ice skate, but she isn't really planning it as a vocation. 'There's something I wanted to be last week,' she said, 'but I've forgotten what it is. I still want to be that if I can remember it.' I had to smile – what a delightful reminder that to her, a whole world of choices lies before her. Wonderful to see life through her eyes again!

There was no doubt in my mind that the two years as part of a complete family group had been good for Jenny. The love and affection that surrounded her brought a closeness with her two young cousins that has remained firmly in place in all the years since. Her going had left a tremendous void in my home life. The two of us had enjoyed a very special relationship, and there was no one else with whom I could share so openly my concerns about her mother. It never crossed my mind that Jenny could be experiencing the same loneliness while she was away, yet as she neared her tenth birthday, she found the courage to go to Elizabeth and tell her that she wanted to come back to live with me.

I had no good news about Margaret when Jenny arrived – once again she had gone missing. As always, the shadow of her illness hung over us both as we rejoiced in our reunion.

12 June 1975

Jenny and I drove down to North Carolina today in a rental car to spend some time with Mother. She is so at loose ends now that Daddy is gone, and I think just having Jenny around will do her good.

Jenny and I both were in a holiday mood as we drove south along the Eastern seaboard states of Pennsylvania, Maryland, and Virginia to reach North Carolina. As I had hoped, Jenny also lifted Mother's spirits, and we stayed with her until early July.

6 July 1975

For the third or fourth time in my life, I am intensely aware of the crouching future just outside the periphery of my vision. It seems to stalk almost every area of my life just now.

My relationship with Michael is, I suppose, most vulnerable. He is such a vital part of my world that it is hard to visualize life without him. Still, marriage seems as elusive as ever. What if his batchelorhood is a permanent part of his character? I really cannot see living the rest of my life in this manner.

And there's Jenny's return. She adds so much to my life, and already colour has come back to some of the black and white matters. Although I really tremble inside at the thought of trying to give her just the right kind and amount of guidance while not squelching her natural growth and development, I'm not really afraid – we'll manage without too much disaster, of that I'm sure.

I still don't have a clue where Margaret is. This has been a longer than usual absence, and I am working very hard on the acceptance the doctors talked about. I do want to be here for her if she should turn up in need of medical help. But I cannot escape the strong feeling that the rest of my own life simply cannot be dedicated to looking after her when she needs me, with long periods of rejection in between.

When Michael turned up at my little flat on a sunny Sunday morning two weeks before August 30, I was shocked to discover that after leaving Jenny and I the night before, he had walked the streets of Manhattan until daybreak wrestling with the question of our future together. In the end, his decision was that we should marry. Having taken such a huge emotional step, he was almost comically anxious to have the deed done. He could hardly wait for Monday, when we could have the required blood tests done and secure a marriage license. As for me, I spent the day in a state of euphoria, and Jenny was beside herself with pure joy.

Michael and I had been introduced in Sardi's restaurant, and since the Ethical Culture Society building was being renovated, we decided to hold our wedding in Sardi's private dining room, which was often used for opening-night reviews of Broadway productions. The Ethical Culture Society leader read marriage vows we had composed ourselves in a lovely ceremony; we were joined by about twenty of our close friends; and in keeping with the setting, Michael raised the toast 'We've opened to rave reviews and we look forward to a lifelong run'. It was a magical evening.

Just how magical our life together turned out to be was brought home with startling clarity during the next school term when Jenny's class was assigned a special project, writing their autobiographies. Jenny's straightforward, matter-of-fact words captured clearly her view of her life and touched me deeply. Despite all the disruptions and emotional upset she had experienced, it said to me that she had come through it all without serious damage to her psyche, as well as how much my marriage to Michael had meant to her.

In February 1976, the *New York Times* published my article on Cork city. A red letter day, and a turning point in my writing career. For the first time, I could present myself unequivocally to the world as a professional writer. A telephone call to the president of Frommer Publishing, which heretofore I would not have had the courage to make, brought my first travel guide-book assignment.

Michael, Jenny and I spent three weeks in Ireland in May and June 1976. Jenny's instant affection for those she met on that trip proved to be a solid foundation of her willingness to enter boarding school there in 1977.

When Elizabeth was hospitalized for major surgery in August 1976, I flew out to Kansas to take care of her and the children during her recuperation. This was a rare opportunity to get to know Jane and Lorenz, and I revelled in our time together. Jenny was happy, too, to be back with them for a time.

6 August 1976
Kids gave me terrific 50th birthday. Pin the tail on the tiger (they didn't have a picture of a donkey!), apple bobbing, lopsided cake, hot dogs, baked beans, etc. Great day.

Three children worked like beavers to prepare a birthday party for me, and they invited all their friends as guests. Really quite wonderful to celebrate reaching the half-century mark in the company of youngsters!

14 August 1976

Dear Ma,

Happy 50th birthday! I'm sorry you couldn't spend it in New York as you always had planned. But at least you made it that far. And you are very much loved by all of us. You've been our rock to cling to. I only wish we could have really done the town for that special occasion. But I know you did the right thing and the only thing that you would have chosen to do, knowing you. I love you more than you'll ever know. So happy 50th birthday, and I'm glad it worked out the way it has. I love you very much. Happy 50th birthday.

Margaret

I didn't know quite what to make of this note. On one hand, it had a return address, so I was relieved to know where she was – or at least, where she had been when the note was written. On the other hand, the frantic outpouring of her love for me and her use of 'Ma' rather than her customary 'Mama' smacked of the onset of another period of psychosis. When I tried to contact her at that return address, she had once again disappeared.

About ten days later, Margaret appeared at my door, dishevelled, dirty, and only a hair's breadth away from hysteria. She adamantly refused to go into a hospital for treatment, insisting there was nothing wrong with her that being 'home' for a while wouldn't cure. Her presence in our little apartment created a lot of tension for Jenny and for Michael, while for me it was like walking on eggs, always fearful of saying or doing the very thing that would send her over the edge.

In early September, I read a newspaper article about the work of the Brain Bio Centre, located just north of Princeton University in New Jersey. Its director was quoted as saying that in addition to stress, alcoholism, depression, arthritis, insomnia, senility, and anxiety, schizophrenia had been cured in nine out of ten of their patients simply through correcting nutritional imbalances. The article went on to explain that it was primarily the undersupply of zinc and oversupply of copper that created those imbalances. It also stressed that success could be achieved only on a case-by-case basis, since each patient's deficiencies are different and there is no general formula for all patients.

I hadn't a clue whether this theory was valid or not, and the article said right up front that it is controversial and most of the mental health profession discounted it. Still, there was that astonishing recovery rate the Centre claimed, and if this kind of approach could help Margaret, I didn't give a fig for conventional psychiatric opinion. When I rang the administrative office and explained her history, they wanted to enrol her immediately as an outpatient. I explained that, based on past experience, I did not believe she would be able to function on that basis and would have difficulty reporting to the Centre each day. It took a few days, but eventually they were able to arrange for her to live on the premises. It was obvious to me that they felt that she would be an excellent example of the miracles they could perform.

> *15 September 1976, 3 a.m.*
> *Just when I had started to believe there might be an answer for Margaret, she's gone again. The people over in Princeton have agreed to take her as a residential member of their orthomolecular clinic research program, even though most of their work is with outpatients. They feel she is the perfect example of what can be accomplished through a vitamins and minerals course of treatment. It wasn't easy to arrange that, and I thought Margaret was looking forward to going. She was to go this afternoon, but last night she went out for cigarettes, and she still has not come back. I will have to let them know later today. Another disappointment. Oh, well, maybe sometime later down the line she will work with them – it would, I think, be a relief for her to have someone feel her problems are physical instead of mental.*

It was December before Margaret turned up again. She had been living in New Jersey, had been hospitalized twice since

August, and was now living with Larry, a man she had met in a bar. In late December, she brought him over to meet us. The phrase 'diamond in the rough' sprang to mind the moment he walked through the door. His weatherbeaten face reflected his outdoor work in the construction trade, and its heightened redness betrayed his hard-drinking lifestyle when he was not working. Instinctively I liked the man. There was a homespun genuineness to him, and it was obvious that he adored Margaret. Hope poked its head up from beneath the layers of hopelessness under which I had buried it.

2 January 1977

Michael, Jenny and I have spent today in Elizabeth, New Jersey, with Margaret and Larry, and my heart is so heavy I cannot think how to lighten it.

For the first time in many years, my Margaret has all the elements to make her happy. Larry truly seems to love her, and she says she loves him. Their apartment is ideal, and gives them something to work on together. She should be well on her way to a lasting happiness. Yet, today, she drank constantly and veered from noisy gaiety to crying jags.

Something about me seems to trigger an instability and a hostility so deep I don't think she even recognizes it as such. Or maybe it is just a fear of disapproval or of failure or something else I can't even imagine.

Whatever the cause, I'd give my life to make her whole. My heart breaks in two with a sound just this side of audible when I see her misery and know I am powerless to prevent it.

It was a miserable day. Margaret and Larry had obviously been drinking before we arrived, but Larry worked hard to keep the conversation going. He also served us a very good dinner, and took loving care of Margaret during her hysterical outbursts and fits of weeping. I was grateful for Michael's strong, un-spoken support for me and for his diplomatic handling of our early departure.

Throughout the day, Margaret had ignored Jenny, who had

adopted a cautious, watchful attitude towards her mother. On the bus ride back to New York, we talked about the day. So many times this kind of exposure to Margaret's illness had been absolutely shattering for us both, and more than anything else I wanted Jenny to feel she could talk about her feelings with me. Today, neither Jenny nor I dissolved into despair, despite our mutual fears for Margaret and the heartbreak of seeing her in such a state. Scar tissue was beginning to form for us both, making the hurt less acute.

By the end of that January, Margaret was back in the upstate New York clinic where she had gone for treatment when she was with James. Larry visited her several times a week and kept us informed of her condition by telephone. It was the first time any of her companions had acknowledged my concerns as her mother. When she was discharged after a relatively short stay, he brought her back to their apartment in Elizabeth.

In June 1977, Jenny and I flew to Ireland, where I attended Writers Week in Listowel, Co. Kerry while Jenny stayed with Evelyn and John Flynn in Cappoquin. I also wanted to talk to Evelyn and other people in our little town about the possibility of Jenny's entering the local boarding school for her remaining school years.

Now twelve years old, she would be entering junior high school in New York City in the autumn. Michael and I, and Jenny herself, had been severely disappointed in her last year's instruction in her Manhattan elementary school. The upcoming transfer would land her in one of the city's most disruptive junior high schools, where academic standards were even lower and where Michael and I both feared for her personal safety.

Irish educational standards are internationally recognized as outstanding, and even though just the thought of living apart from her verged on the intolerable, in view of the New York alternative, we felt the move might be beneficial for Jenny. While she was far from a brilliant student, she had always been eager to learn. During her last year in Manhattan we had watched her begin to lose interest in school when projects on which she had worked long and hard were never even collected by her teacher. Michael had been especially incensed when at the end of the year that same teacher called her by the wrong name. Things were likely to be as bad if not worse in the new school.

By the time September rolled around, Jenny had developed a circle of Irish friends in her age-group; I had held long conferences with the Sisters of Mercy who administered the boarding school; Evelyn had volunteered to keep Jenny on weekends, when boarding school students went home; and Jenny was accepted in St Ann's School. In the years ahead, Evelyn was to become a second mother to Jenny, and the Flynn children took her in as if she were a sister. They gave her the family life I could not.

The tightness that gripped my throat when I left her lasted all through the drive to Shannon Airport and the six-hour flight back to New York. I knew that Evelyn's warm, loving nature was a guarantee that her emotional needs would be recognized and met. I never really doubted the wisdom of the move, but already I missed her. She would be coming home at Christmas, but at that moment it seemed a long wait.

13 September 1977

Dear Granny and Michael,

I had a terrific time at Evelyn's after you left. At school all the girls are very, very nice to me. I'll write again about all the books I have. I am having a terrific time, and I think this is going to be the best year I've ever had!

Love,
Jenny

My spirits soared. Jenny's letter reassured me that her happiness with our decision to send her so far away more than counteracted the loneliness it had brought me.

Chapter Eleven

24 September 1977

Larry and Margaret were married today in New Jersey. I want so much to feel the lifting of a great weight from my shoulders – surely Larry will be able to take care of Margaret from now on. He does seem to love her deeply, and he has seen her through at least one crisis. Still, today Margaret went through the ceremony and the reception that followed (held in the bar where they met) with a stoic, glassy-eyed look except for two crying jags, after which she retreated into that zombie-like expression. I wonder if Larry is aware of the enormous responsibility he has taken on.

It was a sad little wedding. Mingled with my apprehensions, however, was a strong feeling of relief. It was as though at long last I could let go of my responsibility for Margaret and pass it on to Larry. He was different from the other men who had come into her life through the years, with a sort of stability that reassured me that he would take care of her through whatever crisis might loom.

Within a few days, Margaret and Larry had moved to Houston, Texas where the construction industry was booming and Larry would be able to increase his earnings considerably.

10 October 1977

Dear Granny and Michael,

It's great that Mommy and Larry got married, but she did not even write to me! What day did they get married? What did Mommy wear? Did you take any pictures? Do you have their new address? Have you had a letter from Mommy? Has Larry got a job? I know this sounds mean, but I think at least she could have written me a letter. She gets married and then she moves all the way across the country! . . . I guess that means I won't see Mommy at Christmas. I had bought her a Christmas present.

I love you,
Jenny

This excerpt from a long letter from Jenny rang with a deep hurt that made me want to take her in my arms and comfort her. I was deeply touched, and I rang her to promise that we would plan to go down to Houston during the Christmas holidays to visit her mother and Larry.

Chapter Twelve

In September 1977 I began work on my first guidebook for Frommer Publishing. It covered the south-eastern region in which I grew up – the states of Virginia, North and South Carolina, Georgia, and Florida, as well as the city of New Orleans. This was a major turning point for me as a writer. At the age of fifty-one, I felt it was a tremendous personal achievement. Competition is fierce – often cut-throat – in the treacherous world of freelance writing, and I was unashamedly proud of landing this contract. Fees were notoriously small, but the work would allow me to earn my way for the travel I could not afford on my own.

Michael was wonderfully supportive. The book would require extended periods of travel, but when I questioned him about my being away from home so much, he seemed surprised that I would even ask. 'This is your work, Sue,' he said. 'If *my* work meant a lot of travel, would *you* be upset?' I suppose those separations might have been a problem had we not been at our particular point in life when we married. Before we were married, we were both accustomed to being on our own, and the need to be constantly together that is so typical of young love simply was not there for us. Indeed, I firmly believe that emotional dependence on each other has nothing to do with distance apart and that the respect and the space we have always allowed each other have greatly enriched our life together.

Just as I got home from all that travel and was so looking forward to getting into the actual writing of my southeastern book, Michael met me with the news that his mother had fallen and broken her leg. She was at home, but she was alone and immobilized by a plaster cast. He was in a real panic – the doctor had told him her recovery would be slow because of her age (early eighties) and he didn't have a clue how to take care of her. He simply could not take much time off from his work, so there was nothing for it but for me to move out to New Jersey to be with her. It would not be easy to get my book written under these circumstances, but I knew I would have to find a way to manage. And I vowed I would try my best to do it with good grace.

Under the circumstances, there was not a prayer that Jenny and I would be able to fly down to Houston to see Margaret and Larry while Jenny is home for the school holidays. I had made her a firm promise, and I knew she was going to be disappointed. I considered letting her fly down alone, but decided I would wait and see if Margaret was well enough by then for Jenny to go without me.

To say that this was a difficult time is a gross understatement. With Michael away all day, I was left to do all the cooking, fetching, and nursing required by an invalid. At the same time, I was nervous about writing my first book. Any future contract prospects hinged on turning in a well-written manuscript to the publishers, and I pondered every word. That demanded sustained concentration, a virtual impossibility amid constant interruptions. And, when Michael was home, we had very little privacy, so my frustrations found expression only in the pages of my journal. How I missed our little flat in Manhattan!

Jenny was due home from Ireland a few days before Christmas, so I rang Larry to ask about her coming to visit during the holidays. I wasn't surprised to learn that Margaret was back in hospital. During our recent telephone conversations, her high-pitched voice and extravagant protestations of love for me and Jenny had set off the old familiar danger signals. Larry expected her to be released for Christmas Day, but we agreed it was not the time for Jenny to visit on her own. A huge disappointment for Jenny, but she was almost stoic when I explained the situation, and quickly settled into our new environment. She was also a tremendous help to me, taking over much of the to-ing and fro-ing for Michael's mother.

All in all, it wasn't a bad Christmas, with the warmth of our small family unit enhanced by telephone calls to Elizabeth's family and a brief conversation with Margaret. With his usual sensitivity, Michael sensed my cooped-up feeling after such a long confinement in the house whose walls seemed to close in more with each passing day. He quickly arranged to take a day off from work to stay with his mother so that Jenny and I could have a day in Manhattan. He couldn't have given the two of us a better Christmas present! The city becomes a magical place at Christmas, and Jenny had always loved seeing the colourful street and shopfront decorations.

30 December 1977

STUDY SHEDS NEW LIGHT ON

SCHIZOPHRENIA, MANIA, DEPRESSION

Higher than average death rates among persons diagnosed as suffering from these three major psychotic illnesses is one finding of the IOWA 500 PROJECT, the largest single study of its kind done in the nation. Based on a 35-year follow-up study of some 500 patients admitted to University Hospitals between 1935–45 for treatment of the illnesses, the project also includes a study of the patients' families. Male patients diagnosed as suffering from schizophrenia experienced a 4½ times greater

death rate during the first decade after hospitalization compared to the general Iowa population of the same age and sex, and the death rate for women was 3 times higher.
News release from University of Iowa Health News Service

I read with mixed emotions, but little surprise, this item from a medical service which sent periodic news releases to a wide range of writers. Several times during her severe psychotic breaks, I had thought my daughter might well be in the throes of an early death. Indeed, there had been times I would have welcomed for her any relief from the suffering she was enduring. Still, to see this kind of statistic in hard, solid print was a shock. To accept that this would be Margaret's fate would mean abandoning all hope that she would ever find a full, healthy life for herself. Perhaps my own emotional state would have benefited from acknowledging such an indisputable fact. Would her death have provided a final release for *me*? Probably. Yet despite all my years of experience that supported the logic of that acceptance, as Margaret's mother, something in me rejected such an absolute judgement. What is it in a mother, I wondered, that keeps a tiny spark of hope alive when there is none?

10 February 1978

Dear Mama,

Remember how you used to always tell me that you didn't think I really knew how good a person I really was? And how I always believed you were wrong? Well, during my travels and meeting all the people I've met and am living with, I realize I'm a hell of a lot better than I thought. There really are some disturbing people in the world that have twisted, sadistic minds. Garbage or sewage are too good to describe them. But they make the lowest of drunks or tramps look like kings and queens in comparison.

I never felt that bad or good about myself, but from what I've observed (objectively, mind you) my beliefs and ideals beat the shit out of a lot of hypocrites I know.

I guess I'm finally realizing what a real man is, the kind I want, anyway. One with integrity and ideals, and his own person. I love you very much and miss seeing you.

Things are rotten with me and Larry. I guess you would blame that on me, which is really neither here nor there. It's just a lousy situation, no matter what. Am praying for better days to come. Take care of yourself, and I love you very much.

Love,

Margaret

What a shocker this letter was. It was obvious that Margaret was once more sinking into the mental distress that had so many times led to a full psychotic break. This was the first I had heard of any marital problems between her and Larry, but the two references to her love for me and her contradictory assumption that I would blame her were all certain indications of looming trouble. When I rang her during the hours Larry would be at work, her voice betrayed semi-hysteria, and she would only say 'Larry is trying to drive me crazy, when I *know* he is the one doing all those things'. It was impossible to draw any details from her over the telephone, and I ended up simply reiterating my love for her and telling her I would be there whenever she needed someone to talk to. She never called me in the weeks ahead, and I so feared the effect my concern might have on her that I did not ring her again. This was another blow just when I thought my life had settled down for the first time in years. Jenny had flown back to Ireland in early January, and with the holidays behind us, I had finally worked out a routine of invalid care that made time for work on the southeastern guidebook. Now, my thoughts and emotions were so focused on the dangers ahead for Margaret that it was hard going to concentrate on any of the immediate chores that faced me.

It was 20 February before Michael's mother was well enough for me to move back to our own home. By mid-March

I had finished writing the guidebook. To my great relief, the publisher was delighted with the manuscript.

1 February 1978

Dear Granny and Michael,

I forgot to tell you on the phone – I GOT TWO CARDS from guess who? MOMMY!!! One was a lovely Valentine card and the other card said 'When we're together' (on the outside),

'I feel good all over' (on the inside). ISN'T THAT GREAT?!!!

I love you both a lot.

Jenny

A heart-wrenching note in light of Margaret's deteriorating condition. Jenny had had so few evidences of maternal love in the past, it was touching to see just how much those two cards meant to her. For once, there was no need for me to disclose my worries to Jenny. Perhaps, I tried to tell myself, I was reading too much into Margaret's letter and our telephone conversation.

As it turned out, Margaret was in and out of hospital until late March. Larry, who bought into her steadfast denial of schizophrenia, called me to say that he felt she was finally cured of 'her alcohol and drug troubles'. I would have been much more reassured if he could have recognized her schizophrenia and seen that she had treatment for that condition. As long as he deluded himself, my personal sense of relief at knowing that Margaret was now the responsibility of someone else who loved her was greatly lessened by a persistent doubt that she would ever be able to function normally.

Chapter Thirteen

In early April 1978, Paul Pasmantier, president of Frommer Publishing, called and offered me contracts to update Frommer's two guidebooks to Ireland! A miracle – it was more than I could have hoped for to be paid for travelling around Ireland and writing about the places and people there. I was overjoyed, and I decided to share that trip with my mother, in the hope that it would lift for her the loneliness that had engulfed her since my father's death. We travelled the length and breadth of Ireland from early May to mid-July, and such an extended period of togetherness brought out spells of tetchiness I had never seen before in my mother. She and I had always enjoyed each other's company, and it saddened me to be the cause of any irritation for her. Neither of us could have known that cancer had already begun to invade her entire body, which undoubtedly accounted for some of her mood swings.

Despite the occasional unpleasantness between us, I have never regretted our travel together, for by September 1979, cancer had carried her away, and this was the last occasion on which I was to have so much time with her alone.

23 June 1978

A dark cloud descended today on the joy that has brightened my days as Mother and I have travelled around Ireland. When we got back to Cappoquin this evening, a letter from Margaret was waiting. She is back in hospital, this time in the alcohol unit of Austin State Hospital. Thank God for my work! It is a huge relief to be so far away – this time, I don't have to fight the feeling that I should fly right down to Texas to be with her. I wonder should I feel guilty for such an unmotherly reaction? Or does it come under the heading of self-protection? No matter the reasons, however, I cannot deny such a strong emotional response to this new crisis.

And still, I cannot stifle the faint hope that since she is in a state institution, maybe this time there is some hope that she will be transferred to their psychiatric unit, where she can be given proper medication. I keep remembering that the hospital doctor's insistence that alcohol – and drugs, as well – are symptoms of her schizophrenia. Why can't at least one doctor in one of the endless hospitals she has been in recognize that and treat her for the disease instead of the symptoms?

Margaret called me 16 July, and to my intense relief, her voice was strong, with a sound, healthy tone.

20 July 1978

Dear Mama,

I am out of the hospital and am feeling well. Better than I have for a long, long time. Bless Larry's heart, he's been so good through all of this. We have a new apartment now, and it's beautiful! I know you'd love it. It has a pool, air conditioning, and carpet even in the bathroom and kitchen! I'm so proud of it.

Larry and I were hoping maybe you, Michael, and Jenny could come down and stay with us sometime soon. We have plenty of room, and Jenny could swim all she wanted to.

Love,
Margaret

Such a kaleidoscope of emotion packed into so few months since Margaret's letter in February that first signalled trouble between herself and Larry. A familiar pattern of despair followed by hope. This time, however, my overwhelming reaction was one of wariness. I felt a rush of stubborn determination to live my life to the full – I was increasingly unwilling to jeopardize my happy contentment at the turn my own life had taken.

Probably because of the physical distance between Margaret and I, I was able to see the dangers of once more becoming entangled in the web of emotional swings that entrapped my daughter. That is not to say that I did not feel the very strong pull of her invitation to visit so that I could see for myself her true state of mind. After much soul searching, however, Jenny and I together decided that she should spend a week with Larry and Margaret during the summer. Although her visit appeared to have gone well, with no major upsets, Jenny returned to New York with a severe sunburn from the intense Texas sun, and obviously relieved to be back home.

When Margaret's and Larry's wedding anniversary came and went in September and they were still together, my apprehensions were lessened. But not for long. By the end of that month, Larry rang to say that Margaret was once more a patient in the alcoholic unit of the Austin State Hospital. In mid-October, apparently after nothing more than 'drying out' treatment, she was released and back living with Larry. I talked to her on the telephone and wrote a letter that expressed all the support I could muster in the face of my disapproval of what seemed to me a casual dismissal of her fundamental problem.

20 October 1978

Dear Mama,

I just got your letter, and it was so good to hear from you. It was a very consoling letter, and I'm saving it to re-read when I need to.

I went to an AlaNon [an organization for families of

alcoholics] meeting the other night and really enjoyed it. The women there were understanding, although I'm not so sure they liked having an alcoholic woman among them. I plan to go as much as I can.

About Larry, I'm afraid that like a lot of alcoholics, he has more problems than alcohol. They don't come to the surface all the time, but it is obvious to me that they're always there.

Margaret

Margaret arrived in New York on 8 November, telling me that she was leaving Larry because he was still 'trying to drive me crazy'. Kitchen pots and pans disappeared from their customary places, she told me, only to turn up later in the bathroom, closets, or dresser drawers. 'He swears that I am moving them, Mama, and I know that isn't true. And he's been changing the labels on all the spices I like to use. He's just a sadistic son-of-a-bitch, and I can't live with that any more. He wants to put me away in a loony bin, I know he does. I may have my problems with drinking, but I am not crazy'. One more manifestation of the paranoia that had plagued her for so long.

But she had managed to plant a nagging doubt in my mind. After all, I did not know Larry that well, and I had to recognize that he just might have some devious mental quirk that delighted in playing on her vulnerability.

14 November 1978

Dear Granny,

I got your letter telling me about Mommy. I hope she really is OK. I can't help being worried. The first thing I thought when I read she had come to New York because things weren't going too well for her was 'Oh, God, aren't things ever going to go right for her!' It's so unfair.

Lots of love,
Jenny

Chapter Thirteen

Like Jenny, my heart ached for Margaret as once again nothing seemed to go right for her. If she was turning to me for help as she always had, could I possibly refuse her? Surely she had a right to any refuge I could provide for her. And if she was on the verge of another psychotic break, surely it was up to me to see her through it, no matter how disruptive it might be for my own life.

Not one to express his inner thoughts easily, Michael said little the first day or two as Margaret began and ended each day with her litany of grievances and repeated over and over how glad she was to be 'home'. But I could see that he had no patience with her allegations. Finally, in one of our rare moments of privacy when Margaret went out to buy cigarettes, his feelings emerged. 'Face it, Susan,' he told me, 'you've seen her do this to other people, even to you and Jenny. It's always someone else out to get her, never her own mental problems. Can't you see that this is pure fabrication – it's her own twisted way of manipulating you. She wants your approval, always has, and she thinks this is the way to get it.' He put his arms around me and added, with heart-rending tenderness, 'Margaret is thirty years old, for Christ's sake. And she is a very sick girl. Are you going to let her dominate the rest of your life – of *our* life together?' In his love and concern for me, he knew instinctively that I was struggling with an old, familiar fear of saying or doing the wrong thing, and his voice softened as he went on. 'I know that you have to do what you think is right for Margaret, but I don't want to see you hurt again.' Those blessed words momentarily broke through the dreadful isolation of my conviction that Margaret was my problem and mine alone. Still, only I could decide what course to follow – to find a way to help my daughter without destroying my own life.

In the end, I simply listened to Margaret without comment. She was obviously bewildered at my non-reaction to her story – this was the first time I had ever failed to express my complete support and deep love when she was in trouble. As the days went by, she became less agitated, and she finally announced that she had decided to go back to Houston to 'give Larry another chance'. When she left on 18 November, it was with my promise to bring Jenny, now thirteen, down for a visit during the Christmas holidays.

Our two-day Christmas visit was a confusing success – Margaret and Larry were the picture of marital bliss. Margaret radiated an artificial sparkle and raved about all the wonderful things Larry had done for her and how happy they were together. Not a whiff of her paranoia when she was with us in New York!

By early summer 1979, Margaret had again left Larry. My first inkling of this came when she rang to say she had been hired as manager of a rental apartment complex in Houston. The pay was enough for her to live on and included a quite nice apartment on the premises.

9 July 1979

I've just had a sort of confrontation with Jenny, although you can't really call it that because I was the only one involved. There was virtually no response from her.

I know this child very well, and I have always known that it is very hard for her to articulate what she's feeling, and especially when she moves from one environment to another, as is the case now, when she has just come back to New York after a winter in Ireland. The troubling part this time is that there's been no re-connection between us. She is an alien, distant creature, who shows no response to my thoughts, and seemingly has no wish or ability to share her thoughts with me.

I've tried to express all this to her – to tell her what a loss it will be to us both if all the things we've shared in the past don't form the foundation for a feeling of trust and empathy in the rest of our lives. But I honestly don't know if she knows what I've been trying to say to her.

Maybe, as was true with Margaret, I shall have to face the disappointment of knowing that the sensitivity of a very special small child can change so much as to almost disappear during that child's growing up years, particularly the teen years.

Jenny may not be the person I have perceived her to be, and, too, this long period of not being able to write to her or hear from her because of the postal strike in Ireland has created a little gulf that will take time to cross.

Still, it troubles me so much to think of the next few years being just surface ones with the two of us. I've always treasured the workings of her mind and her deep feelings about things – I shall miss knowing what is in her heart if we can't get back to our basis of trust.

It isn't that I don't respect Jenny's right to be a reserved, private person – more than anything else, I want her to grow up knowing who she is and having the courage to be that person. It's just that the coldness – almost rudeness – she is showing now is a personality trait that I find very offensive, and I'm sure others find it so, too.

I shall try as hard as I can to help her see that her present attitude hurts others, and if she still has the feelings for others that has been such a part of her always, that will be enough. If not, then there probably isn't much I can do about it, and I'll simply have to face the fact that she is different from my longtime view of her. If that's the case, then so be it – I'll finish taking care of her until she's grown, and simply try to get over the disappointment and try not to care too much.

For the first time in years, I had to wonder if I had made the right decision when I kept Jenny with me instead of giving her up to a 'normal' life with foster parents. Even when we celebrated her fourteenth birthday the day before the above journal entry was written, she had maintained an aloof coolness that chilled me to the bone. Try as I might to put this personality change down to a teenage phase, I knew in my heart that it had to be faced up to and sorted out. Years before, my mistaken 'behaviour problem' diagnosis had blinded me to the deeper troubles that afflicted Margaret during *her* teen years. I could not let that happen with Jenny.

Had I done the right thing in talking to her so bluntly? Was

I now on the verge of losing this precious child as I had lost Margaret? On that sleepless night, there was no way for me to know. Jenny's strained behaviour the next morning gave no real indication of any change in her attitude, but several times she seemed to be watching me with an expression of bewilderment. Over the next few days, although our confrontational talk was never mentioned by either of us, she gradually relaxed into the warm, loving relationship that had grown so strong over our years together. I didn't even try to analyze what was going on in her head – it was enough that we were close again.

Many years later, she was to tell me what a shock that talk had been for her. For the first time in her young life she had realized what a devastating effect her own behaviour could have on others. 'I never thought for one minute', she said, 'that I could lose *you*, Granny, no matter *what* I said or did. When you said you would take care of my expenses until I was grown, but that was all there would be between us, it scared me to death. I don't know why I behaved as I did that summer, but that talk certainly straightened me out!'

Jenny had decided to spend part of her summer holiday in Houston with Margaret, but her two weeks turned into a nightmare of confinement in Margaret's air conditioned apartment as temperatures soared above 100 degrees. Once again, Jenny seemed relieved to get back to New York. A scant week after her return, a Houston hospital notified us that Margaret had been admitted for treatment for alcoholism and had lost her job. I wondered, but did not linger on it, if Jenny's leaving had brought on this setback. As usual, she was back out of the hospital and living on welfare funds within a very short time.

17 September 1979

Greenville, North Carolina
Marie [the youngest of my two sisters] called this morning to say that Mother was operated on this morning for gallstones and is riddled with cancer through all her major organs. Doctors say there is no hope of recovery. What a terrible shock!

Chapter Thirteen

I was lucky to get an early evening flight, and I am booked into a Greenville motel – not so much driving back and forth to Bethel [the town in which my mother had been living since my father's death], and it will be a refuge of privacy as other members of the family arrive. Louise is flying down from New Jersey early tomorrow morning.

No way to tell just how long we have left to be with Mother – to let her know just how grateful all three of us are to her for our happy childhood home life. For me, there is also a good measure of regret that I haven't been able to provide that for my girls. The hospital here bent their visiting hours to let me see her for about a half hour tonight, even though it was so late. Hard to leave her. From now until the end, I think we should arrange with the hospital for one of us to be with her at all times.

Exactly one week later, Mother died at 4 a.m. It is impossible to put into words the impact of her leaving on my sisters and I. It is hard to realize that both my parents were gone. Louise and Marie and I drew much closer than we had been for many years. Still, it was not the same. We had lost the two anchors that had kept us safe all our lives.

24 September 1979

Margaret is coming by bus from Houston and seemed upset on the phone that she hadn't been notified of Mother's illness earlier so she could have had time with her then. Maybe I should feel a bit of guilt at that, but I simply cannot, and as awful as it sounds – even to me – I am uneasy about her coming for the funeral. I'll just have to wait and see and pray that this kind of strain will not bring on another psychotic break.

As is true with every funeral, the next two days were hectic and exhausting. Margaret, however, turned out to be a real asset. Her native charm came to the fore – she was the perfect hostess for friends and family when I was busy with burial details. It

137

was touching to hear her express how much her grandparents had meant to her. Even more touching for me was her deep feeling for our extended family and her need to be a part of it. It would have been the easiest thing in the world to be seduced into believing that she had turned a corner and that this sweetness – so much a part of her early childhood – was back to stay.

She stayed with me in North Carolina until 2 October and our bonding as we worked to close up Mother's house is one of my most treasured memories of that sad time. That memory stands alone, untainted even by the 10 October call to tell me she was back in hospital in Houston.

Chapter Fourteen

7 January 1980

Dear Mama,

I got a letter from Jenny today and answered it tonight. I told her how proud I was of her for choosing psychiatric nursing as a career. There is so much good you can do for people in despair, and I believe she has the kindness and compassion that it takes to do a good job.

Of course, I really wish Jenny would decide to come home and finish school and maybe even live with us. I think about how much fun it would be to have her with us all the time. Of course, I realise that is only selfish thinking. I really only want for her what she wants, as long as it is not harmful for her.

Love,
Margaret

When she left the Houston hospital in mid-December, Margaret had gone back to live with Larry, and this letter was filled with details of their happy Christmas. They had driven to Austin for

Margaret to deliver small gift packages she had put together for twenty patients in the State Hospital's alcoholism unit.

Her obvious pleasure in this kind of practical compassion was a reaffirmation of the *real* Margaret I had always known lived just beneath the veneer of schizophrenia. Tears sprang to my eyes, and for the umpteenth time I willed her to ward off assaults of that terrible disease and to hold on to her true self. Was it my too-eager imagination that read into her empathy with 'people in despair' and psychiatric nursing an oblique recognition that she could be counted among their ranks? That her problems went beyond alcohol and drugs?

23 January 1980

Dear Granny and Michael,

Granny, if I write to Mommy about how she's feeling about all the years she's missed with me . . . Well, never mind, I'll try!!!

Oh yes, don't worry, I'm not considering psychiatric nursing because I feel obligated to do it because of Mommy (that really would be a waste of time, wouldn't it?). At the moment I want to, but only time will tell whether that feeling will stay. Anyway, I don't know if I have the guts or the emotional stability (I think that's how you would phrase it) or strength.

Lots of love,
Jenny

In early summer, Margaret rang to say she had left Larry and found a job as manager of another apartment complex. This time, she insisted, the separation was for good. That did, indeed, prove to be the case, but to this day, I don't know if they ever went through the formality of a divorce.

Before the end of 1980, Margaret was once again admitted to the alcoholism unit of Austin State Hospital, and she rang just three days before Christmas to say she would be undergoing minor surgery the next day to remove a growth on her cervix for a biopsy. Her voice was relatively calm, even though she said that if the growth proved to be malignant, she would then face major surgery for cervical cancer.

Christmas Day, 1980

Dear Mama, Jenny, and Michael,

Mama, thank you so much for calling today. You made me really feel good. I hope I won't have to have any more surgery, but if I do, I'm not so sure I can be brave about it, being that it's a much bigger operation, and it sure would be a good time to have my mother here with me to hold my hand or whatever. I don't want you to go into debt to get down here, though. Promise?

I went into the hospital Monday afternoon and got back over here yesterday afternoon. I didn't know they were going to do a D&C, but it was OK, because I'm sure I could use one. I really couldn't believe how good I felt through the whole thing. I was out of bed walking around within about two hours. Some of the patients from over here came to see me both days, and we had a ball.

Today around here has been good. Just a bunch of sober drunks running around cutting up and sharing with each other. There's really a lot of love between recovering alcoholics. I guess we feel if we don't care about us, no one else will. We all know that isn't true, though. It's a fun Christmas, the first I've ever had in the hospital, and little or no depression in the air.

Please tell Jenny I'm sorry there are no presents from this end this year. But it won't always be that way. I believe that. It seems that it's been one thing after another in the last few months, and very confusing sometimes. I love her very much and am very proud of her.

If the biopsy comes out OK, I won't call, and if it isn't I'll call you as soon as I know.

Love and kisses,
Margaret

The biopsy proved to be malignant, and surgery was scheduled for 7 January. Jenny flew back to Ireland on 3 January and on the 5th I flew to Austin to be with Margaret. I found her still in the alcoholism unit and learned that her surgery had been postponed for a few days. Then, on 12 January, the doctors informed me that, despite the urgency of the operation, it would have to be put even further back. Because of her prolonged drinking, Margaret's general physical condition had so deteriorated that they could not risk surgery until she was in better health. They planned to keep her there and build up her strength before setting a new surgical date, so the next day I returned to New York, where a guidebook deadline still had to be met.

26 January 1981

Margaret rang last night to say she will have the operation tomorrow, so today I flew back down to Austin and was able to visit with her in the evening.

She is putting on a brave face and chatted away as though my visit were just a social call. Underneath it all, she is pretty scared, and I am glad I could come down to be with her.

Margaret's surgery was scheduled for 1 p.m., and I waited for about three hours before learning that it was completely successful, with 98% chance of non-recurrence. Such a relief.

I wasn't able to see Margaret after the operation, so returned to the hotel. I was bursting to tell someone – *anyone* – the good news, but neither Elizabeth nor Michael answered the phone, even though I rang them several times.

The following day, I was only allowed to visit Margaret between 1 and 4 pm. She seemed a bit dispirited, but had brightened up somewhat by the time I had to leave. For me, it was a long day that ended with dinner in my hotel room and several hours of television, and I resolved to spend my idle time exploring Austin, about which I knew precious little during the three days until my return to New York on 31 January. In the end, I spent most of that free time on University of Texas campus, examining original typescripts of D. H. Lawrence and other writers of that calibre. One of the few copies of the historic Gutenberg bible is also lodged here, and I wished for my newspaper father (who always called himself a simple printer) to share with me the thrill of seeing one of the first products of a printing press with moveable type. My afternoons were spent with Margaret, whose recovery was progressing at a faster pace than doctors had expected.

17 February 1981

The New York Times *today carried a lengthy article that focused on such recent publications as Mark Vonnegut's* The Eden Express, Autobiography of a Schizophrenic Girl *by a patient known as Renée, and* Life/Time *articles by clinical psychologist Jane Rittmayer. In each case, the study found that a diagnosis of schizophrenia was misleading, even though each patient had displayed some symptoms of the schizophrenic. It blamed imprecise diagnostic criteria for such misleading of doctors, patients, and the reading public.*

Made me think. Could Margaret's insistence that she is not mentally ill actually be closer to the truth than the earlier diagnoses of schizophrenia? Could it be that her problems really are due to alcoholism and drugs? I keep remembering the doctor's explanation that hallucinations can be drug induced.

What am I to think? Well, I just don't know, and if the medical specialists I've looked to for help are so confused, what hope is there for me to understand what has happened and is happening to my daughter.

Over the two years immediately following her discharge from hospital, Margaret found and lost work as a sales clerk and radio dispatcher for an Austin taxi company; came to New York for several weeks between jobs; was hospitalized just eight days after moving in with Elizabeth in South Carolina; and made her way back to Austin. My journals during that period are filled with addresses for her in Austin and notices that my letters could not be delivered to her. Weeks and months passed during which I had no way of reaching her and had to wait for her to contact me.

I have often thought I would have lost my mind during this time of ups and downs and long silences had it not been for my work. I was now writing six travel guidebooks. Each covered a two-year span, and I had arranged to update three each year. The travel, and above all the marvellous overseas friends I made, were life-saving diversions from my ever-present anxiety about Margaret.

On 24 February 1983, Margaret arrived from Austin in the evening. Her dishevelled clothing, horrid makeup, wild-eyed expression, and high-pitched voice made it painfully clear that she was very sick. She had been living on the street in Austin, and I never learned just how she managed to get to New York. I knew immediately that she was in desperate need of help beyond any I could provide.

She went straight to bed, but slept little during the night, and I had an almighty struggle to convince her the next morning that she *must* get to a hospital.

When we finally did get to see a young intern, he took one look at her eyes, and brusquely announced that we would have to come back the next day for a consultation with a senior member of the medical staff. A shortage of beds precluded their keeping her overnight. With no trace of compassion or understanding for Margaret, he was already reading the chart of the next patient as we were quickly shunted out the door.

How on God's earth was I to see her safely through the night and get her back to the hospital in the morning? I knew with a dreadful certainty that her stubborn denial of mental illness made that impossible. In the present confusion of her mind, there was no way she was going to respond to logic, but in one last, futile attempt to get through to her, I asked why she had come home to me if she was unwilling to accept my judgement.

The look of utter disdain she turned on me then is forever emblazoned on my memory. With scathing contempt, she replied, 'Don't you understand, Mama, I had no choice!'

26 February 1983
Margaret in bed all day. She insists she isn't mentally ill and refuses to return to hospital or to take the medication they gave us last night. I tried my best to persuade her that she wouldn't hesitate to take an aspirin or a painkiller to relieve the temporary symptoms of a physical illness until a permanent cause can be diagnosed and treated – it is really silly to deny herself the same kind of temporary easing of the emotional pain she is so obviously suffering. Her only reply is that although it might make her look and act better, in her words, 'That medication is like a straight-jacket – I always feel the same inside, I just can't express my feelings'. Kept bedroom dark all day and shouted at me to 'Get out and leave me alone' when I tried to take her some food.

Can't help but wonder if her condition creates any physical danger for Michael and I.

My heart gradually froze with fear as Margaret's behaviour became more and more hostile towards Michael and I. A mother's worst nightmare: to be physically afraid of her own child!

Over the next two days, each time I walked into the darkened bedroom, I found her either carrying on a conversation with voices that were inaudible to me or holding forth in long discourses about how much she loved Austin and how she longed to be back there. The wildness in her eyes never abated, and finally I had to face the fact that I could no longer cope with this situation. The only solution I could come up with was to get her back to Austin and pray that someone or some social agency would come up with the help she so desperately needed.

28 February 1983
Gave Margaret cheque for $2,000 and put her on plane for Austin. My heart is broken, and I don't know what else to do.

Margaret's change in mood and attitude when I told her of my decision was astonishing. Docility shut out hostility, and there was a hint of gaiety in her manner as she lay in bed watching me sort and pack the jumble of clothes she had brought with her.

These terse journal entries chronicle an episode that will haunt me all my life. Try as I might to console myself with the thought that I was at least sending her away with clean clothes and enough money to meet her immediate needs, I was consumed by a terrible feeling that I was actually doing the unthinkable, turning away my own child and *paying* her to go.

11 March 1983

Dear Mama,

Well, I'm sure you know I arrived safely. I'm sorry I was unable to socialize the way I would have liked to, but I'm sure you understand.

I'm writing mostly to thank you for the wonderful way you straightened out my things and all the love I know went in it. It was wonderful to unpack and feel all the motherly love that you put into all that work.

I'm so sorry about all the expenses you're having to go to, and as soon as I marry a rich husband, I'll pay you back.

Please tell Michael I'm sorry for all the inconvenience and thank him for being so sweet and understanding.

I'm still feeling pretty bad, but that's par for the course.

Love,
Margaret

My relief at having some word from Margaret after sending her away prompted me to send an immediate reply via telegram to the address shown in her letter rather than wait a few days for a letter to reach her. The very next day, however, a notice from Western Union informed me, 'We are sorry your telegram number 4-0732895122 is undelivered for the following reason: Addressee moved, present address unknown' – a message that was to be all too familiar in the years to come.

Chapter Fourteen

In a desperate attempt to put this emotional kick in the stomach away and get on with the life I was making for myself as a writer, I threw myself into my work. Travel imposed a physical distance from the pain of not knowing Margaret's whereabouts – at home in New York the conviction was inescapable that I should be able to do more to make her life easier, as well as the awful memory of having turned her away.

There was no further word from Margaret until early December.

2 December 1983

Dearest Margaret,

I'm so sorry that $100 is all I can scrape together just now. I know it won't last long, but it's the best I can do.

My heart is with you, Margaret, and I haven't been able to stop thinking of you and praying that somehow you'll work back to a good living arrangement. You've always been so strong, and that gives me faith that you'll get through this bad time as you have all the others. I'd give my very soul if there were some way I could help you do that, but we're both experienced enough now to know that if there is such a way we haven't been able to find it yet.

In the meantime, just hold on tight to your belief in yourself and the knowledge that I love you more than words would ever express. Please call whenever you feel like it, and be sure to let me know where and how you are – not knowing is agony!

All my love,
Mama

This letter was sent to the Salvation Army hostel in Austin, and since it was not returned, I had to assume that Margaret was there when it arrived. When I rang there the next week, however, the attendant on duty was almost rude when he told me she had left and they did not know how to reach her.

Throughout 1984, there were periodic telephone calls from her, new addresses, and long silences.

That summer was especially significant for Jenny. Now nineteen years old, she had decided that psychiatric nursing was not, after all, the career for her and was enrolled in a commercial course. During the past year, she had fallen in love with Seán, and in August, he came over to New York to ask Michael and me for her hand – a delightful, Old World custom that I thought was long gone. Although I had met him when I was in Ireland, it was during his two-week stay with us that both Michael and I grew to know, respect, and love him. His love for Jenny and hers for him was a joy to behold, and their sensible decision not to marry for a year or two was reassuring. Jenny's disappointment that we could not reach her mother to tell her about the engagement was the only sadness of those two weeks.

Seán's parents owned a small guesthouse, restaurant, and pub and were looking forward to Seán and Jenny running it when they married. Jenny was understandably nervous about cooking and serving meals for guests, but the internationally renowned Ballymaloe Cookery School, located just twenty miles from Cappoquin, accepted her for their three-month residential course. Their curriculum covered such basics as planning, shopping, cooking, and presentation – exactly what she would need to know. All her qualms had vanished in a blaze of self-confidence by the time she completed the course.

On 18 March 1986, I came across a newspaper article that held a welcome bit of information. 'The architecture and chemistry of the brains of schizophrenics,' it read, 'can be actually different from those of normal people, new studies show. As a result, a revolution in psychiatry has occurred in which biology has become the main focus of the research on this most devastating and intractable disease of the mind.

'Among the most dramatic differences revealed in the new research are computer-generated images of the brain that light up in vital regions when a normal person tackles a mental problem. These regions stay ominously dim when the disordered mind of the schizophrenic takes the same test.' It went on to state that while physical brain abnormalities have long been suspected among schizophrenics, these abnormalities have only recently been pinned down by researchers using new tools for exploring the brain. 'The new evidence indicates that the disease is far more than a consequence of adverse familial, social and other environmental experiences as many American psychiatrists long believed. Some scientists still maintain that these biological changes may be results rather than a cause of the disease. But many biological psychiatrists today speak bitterly of the pain the earlier view inflicted on the families of schizophrenics, adding guilt to the agony of watching a spouse or child turn into an irrational, angry or apathetic stranger.'

What a change in attitude! That article went a long way towards easing the guilt that refused to go away completely. Unfortunately, I could find no hint in the piece of any medical strategy to correct those brain differences – no word of being any closer to a cure. Still, every little bit of understanding of the nature of the disease moves the possibility of effective treatment that much closer. Best of all, this piece got parents – especially mothers – off the hook as a cause of schizophrenia.

As months went by with no word from Margaret, I frantically called every contact number I had ever had in Austin, from the state hospital to the taxi company where she once worked to one of the social welfare agencies. Not one had any record of her whereabouts.

15 November 1986

Dear Jenny,

You've been on my mind a lot lately. There is so much I want to say to you, and if I were not trying to watch the bills, I'd telephone you for a long chat.

From the time you came to live with me, what I have wanted for you most has been the things that will let you lead a full, rewarding life with as much real happiness – happiness based on the lasting things – as possible, and the strength and courage to meet the problems that make that kind of happiness even more to be treasured. Bless you, you've always been the kind of girl who grasped the essentials, sometimes even before I did, and although we've been through some rough (and funny) ups and downs, things have turned out pretty well, and I think you're well able to cope with whatever comes up and glean the happy parts of living from all the troublesome parts.

For so many years, I've had to decide as best I could what would be best for you, but for the past few it has been up to you to chart your own direction, and I have just tried to let you know you have my love and support in the things you wanted to try. Right now, you've made a decision concerning life with Seán that makes me very, very happy and gives me a sense of security about your future, and I hope with all my heart that you feel more and more sure about that yourself. I love you more than you will ever know, except perhaps when you feel the same for your own children.

The one thing I've always wanted most to give you – a sound, well mother – has never been possible, but it has meant the world to me that you have understood that it has been as much a tragedy for me as for you that she has suffered so. And I know, too, that you feel as I do that at some time in the future that may change, and I know you will always pray for that to happen, as I do.

I miss having you close by to say this kind of inside stuff to you face to face. Just know, as I am sure you do, that even my mistakes have been made out of love!

All my love always,
Granny

Seán and Jenny had set their wedding date for early April, which brought down over my head such an avalanche of

Chapter Fourteen

unspoken sentiments that I felt a real compulsion to write this letter to Jenny.

On the day of her wedding in Cappoquin, Jenny was radiant, glowing with happiness, and my heart nearly burst with love for her. This much, at least, I had been able to do for Margaret. How I wanted her to be with us.

Chapter Fifteen

21 June 1987
Margaret arrives 5:13 p.m. It's a little after 1pm – another hour-and-a-half before I can leave to meet her plane at JFK, and it seems an eternity. Mother would say I'm jumping out of my skin, and she wouldn't be too far wrong. Just cannot settle down to anything in this little lost space in time.

When Margaret called from Austin last night about 9:30pm, never have I felt such a rush of relief and pure joy. Just to know she is alive after nearly two years of not being able to find her is almost more than I could have hoped for, even though I've always known she's a survivor.

Thank God – or whatever it is that prompts intuition to prod so insistently it cannot be ignored – I cancelled the press trip to Morocco for no other reason than that prodding, otherwise I would not have been here for her call.

And now, as I wait for the time I can leave to meet her, my emotions are swirling right back to all the other times of crisis in her life when it collides with mine. The deep, raw inner wound of having to send her away when last she came has not healed, as I thought, but has been simply waiting to gush forth blood afresh.

What will I say to her? Can I find words that won't wound her or make her feel guilty for not letting me know how and where she's been? And what state will she be in? Of one thing I am certain: she is in dire straits, else that phone call would never have been made. Whatever the straits, I only pray that this time I can be for her what she so desperately needs me to be and has needed me to be for all her 39 years.

The part of me that is quick to spot irony looks back with astonishment at my bold proclamation when Jenny was married: 'For the first time in 42 years I'm responsible only for myself – this is my own personal Independence Day!' What arrogance! I think now that responsibility must come right along with the first breath we draw – babies responsible for learning, juveniles responsible for maturing, lovers responsible for their lovers, parents responsible for children (and many time for grandchildren), and grandparents responsible for their own welfare so as not to be a burden on their children.

And with it all, we must every one have a certain responsibility to try as hard as we can to make some sense of it all.

As Margaret came through the arrivals doorway, my heart sank. She was barely recognizable – a skeletal figure dressed in dirty tee-shirt, scruffy jeans, and worn sandals partially covering grimy feet. Most heartbreaking of all for me was her garish, badly applied makeup, always a dead giveaway of serious mental trouble. Wearing the broad, artificial smile I knew so well she rushed into my arms, gushing thanks for sending the airfare.

She looked as if she hadn't eaten in days, so we headed for the airport restaurant. The hostess looked at Margaret with an expression of total disgust and seemed doubtful that we could be seated. My instant, unexpected reaction was 'If she thinks I am going to be embarrassed out of providing my daughter with a decent dinner, she has another thing coming', and I was quite prepared to call for the manager. She must have seen the steely anger that swept over me, for she quickly led us to a corner table, where Margaret gulped down a hot meal.

In the taxi going home, I learned she had been living on the streets of Austin for most of the two years since I last heard from her. She also told me she had been hospitalized in January for severe burns all down one thigh and leg incurred when she had slept too close to a fire she had built in an abandoned building against the bitter cold of a Texas winter. At home, I was appalled at the huge purplehued scar exposed when she undressed to fall into bed.

For the next few days, Margaret slept long hours and spent her waking hours restlessly prowling our apartment. It was impossible to break through her surface cordiality for any sort of meaningful conversation, and she had little to say beyond 'I had no choice but to call you, Mama' and 'I can only stay two weeks'. Before the week was out, however, she began leaving the apartment in the early afternoon, and returning in the early evening in time for dinner. She would only say that it was good to be back in New York and that she was going for a walk around the city. When I offered to walk with her, she flatly refused, and she was secretive about just where in the city she was walking. Where *did* she go, I wondered. Was she meeting someone on the streets? By the second week, she had become more and more withdrawn, and her sparse comments were delivered with a curtness that bordered on hostility. While she was certainly not psychotic at that time, the mystery of what was going on in her mind and her behaviour towards Michael and I fostered a fear that she might be on the brink of another psychotic break and that our safety might actually be in danger.

Despite my apprehensions, when Margaret repeatedly insisted she only could stay two weeks, the thought of her returning to her street life in Austin through the coming winter was intolerable. Reminding her of the hardships she had endured the past winter, I tried to prevail on her to stay with us at least through the cold months. My own fears notwithstanding, I thought that if I could persuade her to stay, I could at least get medical help when and if she needed it. Her only reply, however, was 'You *know* that isn't possible, Mama. I *have* to go back to Austin'. Still, the second week came and went and each day there was no mention of exactly when she would leave.

I was in a quandary as the third week wore on, for I was committed to leave on 9 July for several weeks' research on my New Zealand guidebook. To break my contract and cancel the trip would mean forfeiting the advance, a financial loss we really could not afford. When Margaret overheard me discussing this dilemma with Michael, she burst into the room and ran to put her arms around me, protesting in a voice dripping with synthetic sweetness that I should not let her being there interfere with my work. 'I will be all right here with Michael until you get back,' she insisted. No mention of having to leave.

With my heart in my throat, I packed my bags and headed for the airport. I will never know if this was one of my worst mistakes or if cancelling the book contract and remaining in New York would have made any difference.

9 July 1986

Michael,
    I'm on my way back to Austin. Thank you so much for your patience. Tell Mother I love her very, very much.

Love,
Margaret

P.S. I love you, too.

When I rang Michael in response to the message waiting for me at my Auckland guesthouse, he told me he had found Margaret's note when he returned from seeing me off at the airport. Neither of us had any idea then, nor have we ever learned, just how she planned to travel from New York to Austin.

She was gone, and it would be eight long years before I had word of her again.

Chapter Sixteen

The next year, 1988, Margaret's disappearance took on another dimension when my New York physician diagnosed lumps as breast cancer and stressed the urgency of an immediate mastectomy. When the only surgeon available to us under our medical insurance refused to perform even preliminary biopsies for a full five weeks, I flew to Dublin and in sixteen days had undergone both the biopsies and the removal of my left breast.

Cancer is a scary thing at best. At the age of sixty-two, for the first time ever it brought me face to face with my own mortality. While the major surgery I faced is more or less routine these days, there was always the possibility that I might not have survived the operation or that the disease might have spread so widely that it would prove impossible to remove all the diseased tissues. Both possibilities do tend to focus your mind.

It had long been my firm conviction that death is simply an extension of life – life's last great adventure – and that one cannot savour life to the fullest without a recognition of death.

That belief was not shaken in the least, but now that I could well be embarking on that adventure in the immediate future, every facet of my life was thrust into new perspective. What would become of Margaret if I were gone? To whom could she turn when she 'had no choice' but to ask for help, albeit only the temporary help I had been there to give in the past? And if no one could find her to let her know what had happened, what would the shock of my dying do to her fragile emotional psyche?

As it turned out, although I went into shock on the operating table and woke up trussed from head to toe in an aluminum shock blanket (I shall forever empathize with the Christmas turkey as it is shoved into the oven with just such a covering!) the operation was a complete success. The kindness that accompanies the highest medical standards of hospital care in Ireland was a revelation to me. Not a trace of the impersonal efficiency that is the hallmark of so many large American hospitals. When I went home to our little house in Cappoquin, everyone I knew in this small town, and many I had not even met, conspired to speed my recovery with that same extra-ordinary kindness. My heart swelled with pure love for this blessed country and its people, and my resolve to make this my permanent home as soon as possible grew even stronger.

Excerpt from the Letters to the Editor feature, February 1989 issue, Atlantic Magazine.
The overwhelming weight of research evidence over the past twenty years supports the view that the chronic mental illnesses at issue (principally schizophrenia) originate in physical malfunctions of the brain itself. The symptoms are craziness, but the illness is a malfunctioning organ of the body (part of the brain). This is a medical problem – as sure as diabetes, heart trouble, or whatever – having literally nothing to do with psychiatry. The treatment of choice is medication to control psychosis, plus support and counselling to adjust to what is usually a lifelong handicap. Imagine treating heart

trouble or diabetes or myopia with psychotherapy or family systems therapy!

It is difficult to exaggerate how awful the experience is – struggling alongside an invariably bright and gentle young adult who gradually loses the ability to reason and gradually descends into lunacy.

The persistence of 'bad family' notions wreaks widespread damage in mistreatment, millions of dollars of wasted research money, ineffective mental health services and casual, if unintended, cruelty to families already anguished and overstressed by a psychotic in their midst.

I could have kissed the person who wrote that letter! In all the years of Margaret's illness, this was the strongest statement I had encountered of the hurt inflicted on families of schizophrenics by such a large proportion of the medical profession. His letter mirrored the anger that had so often consumed me and had been unable to express except in the pages of my journal. That letter should be required reading for every medical professional dealing in any capacity with mental illness.

10 July 1989

All day I have been trying to shake off the vivid imagery of the nightmare last night that left me in a cold sweat and shaken to the core. I seemed to be standing on a high, rocky cliff made slippery by spray from huge, angry sea waves crashing halfway up its face. Just beyond my reach, a monstrous sea turtle gripped Margaret with its two front feet high above the clifftop. As I watched in horror, the serpentine head bent over her struggling figure and tore away the entire back of her skull. Her anguished 'Mama-a-a-a' still rings in my ears tonight as it has all day.

I don't need a dream analyst to tell me where that nightmare came from – the feeling of utter helplessness and futility that has never lifted since the last time Margaret walked away from home weighed more heavily yesterday when I remembered that it was on July 9, exactly two years ago, that she left.

What I have to wonder is whether or not this hellish dream is an omen that wherever she is, Margaret is once more calling out in desperation for help from me. I know that thought borders on the ridiculous, but it is not beyond the realm of possibility that she does need my help and is for some reason, physical or emotional, unable to get in touch.

Will I ever hear from her again? My strongest emotion tonight is one of grief. I know in my heart that she is a survivor, but with the sights and sounds of that nightmarish dream so hellishly vivid I don't know that she is able to survive the monster of schizophrenia that has been tearing her apart all these years. And if she should lose that struggle, how am I to know when I don't know where she is?

For months, I relived that horrid dream, and while the memory of it has faded a bit over the years, from time to time I still have flashes of its vivid detail.

10 November 1989

Michael went by 94th Street today to collect the mail and found a bill from the hospital for Margaret. It shows admission and discharge on October 21. I called the hospital and after a long hassle talked to someone in the Records Room, who could give me no real details, only that she had received 'treatment' in their Emergency Room and it was not considered necessary to keep her overnight. The charge is $145, but the bill doesn't specify for what.

I can't help but wonder if she were in NYC on the streets when I had such a strong feeling for street people on 15 October.

Could she have been sending out mental 'Help' signals?

When we had recently moved from our Manhattan apartment into a smaller, less expensive apartment in Long Island City in order to divert more of our moderate income towards an eventual move to Ireland, some mail continued to escape the forwarding address net of the postal service, so Michael periodically checked

160

the Manhattan mailbox. The mystery of Margaret's in-and-out visit to the hospital has never been solved. I will never know if she went first to our Manhattan address and took herself to the hospital when she discovered we had moved. There was no way, of course, she could have known our new address, but had she tried to telephone me, she would have been given our new number, a service the telephone company agreed to extend an extra year in view of the situation with Margaret.

The following years found me working hard to get on with my life and deaden as much as possible the acute pain of my younger daughter's illness. It was beyond me, however, to hold fast to what was the only bulwark I had between me and that awful hurt. Periodically, I yielded to an irresistible urge to find her and telephoned every agency in Austin with whom she might have had some contact. Always, it was an exercise in futility.

Despite the worry about Margaret that never completely left me, my own life during those years was filled with positives. The birth of Jenny's two daughters, the continuing expansion of my travel writing into periodicals as well as guidebooks, and longer and longer periods of living in Ireland to prepare for the time Michael would retire and join me there, all were ingredients of a contentment that augured well for the years remaining to me.

Then, in my sixty-ninth year, came the letter from Sarah McCoy quoted in Chapter Two of this book. Margaret was found, and Jenny and I rushed to Austin.

Chapter Seventeen

Although Jenny and I were earlier getting in to JFK than scheduled, Michael was there waiting. Never, I think, had I been so glad to see him! And it had nothing to do with his bringing funds. It was just knowing that he knew all about this situation and all that lay behind us that was such a comfort. We settled in in the upstairs lounge, had a snack and a few drinks. Jenny, sensitive soul that she is, insisted on browsing through the shops and giving us time on our own, a lovely thing to do that Michael and I both appreciated, even though we both felt perfectly free to speak our minds and hearts in front of her – always had. Funnily enough, I would have given the world to make love with Michael before heading off – don't know how sex could rear its head at such a time, but it would have, I think, just solidified the wonderful feeling of support and security I felt with him. I really hated to leave him.

The hour-and-a-half wait between planes in Dallas airport seemed endless before we boarded a smaller plane for the short flight to Austin. Although by local time our arrival there was

Chapter Seventeen

only 11p.m., because of the time difference, it had now been 21 hours since we had left Cappoquin.

As Sarah had promised, two members of Alcoholics Anonymous were there to meet us. They drove us to the Red Roof Inn, a budget motel on the outskirts of the city, where Sarah had booked us a room. When they asked if they should try to find Margaret that night and bring her to the motel, simultaneously, we told them we were so exhausted that we would rather see her the next day. They looked relieved, and said that since she was usually drinking at night and wandering on the streets, they hadn't known in what condition they would find her. They were two lovely young women and seemed to be completely unjudgemental.

After a hot bath, Jenny and I fell into bed. As tired as I was, I slept very fitfully, and every time I woke up, Jenny was also awake. It was hot as Hades, for one thing, and although we both found the air conditioner stultifying, it was impossible to leave it off. Once or twice, we went outside for a smoke, until the heat (about 100 degrees F even at night!) drove us back in. Again, I was so conscious of just how much it meant to me to have Jenny with me – suppose I were doing this on my own!

The next day, Sarah brought Margaret over to the motel about 11 a.m. My heart sank when I saw her. Skin and bones doesn't *begin* to describe her skeletal appearance. She was wearing a ragged pair of cutoff blue jeans (very short) over a black bathing suit, and had I seen her in my compulsive searching of faces of the homeless, I truly don't think I'd have known her. She had always been small, but she seemed tiny now. Her hair was thin, straggly, and pulled back severely from her face, which was so wizened that there was hardly a trace of the sweetness and beauty that it had always reflected, even when she was deep in the clutches of a psychotic break. She looked far older than her forty-seven years, battered by her illness and the life she had led.

An artificial sweetness came over her features when she greeted us, and almost without exception a wide smile was

163

plastered on her face when either of us talked to her directly –
the heartbreak came when a sad, almost grim, look closed
down the smile the moment any one conversation ended. Try
as I might, I could not reach behind either of those facades and
find the Margaret whose words, expressions, and actions came
from her heart.

Later that night, Jenny expressed it precisely when she said
it was as if Margaret were 'on auto pilot all the time'.

It did, however, seem to mean the world to her that we had
come so quickly, and I was glad Jenny had insisted on that.
Margaret kept repeating that she just could not believe how
soon we had come – surely, I thought, she must know how
much both of us love her and what deep concern we have had
for her these past eight years.

Her clothes were so pitiful that my first thought was to get
her decently clothed, so we took a taxi (our motel was so far out
the highway that every taxi ride cost $12 or $15 plus tips, and
there was no public transportation) to the nearest shopping
mall. I will never forget that taxi ride – Margaret kept up a
constant stream of talk about her street life: three times raped
by the same black man; another homeless man giving her a pair
of glasses he had stolen; her dependence on a garage owner for
the abandoned car that had been her home; her high regard for
the police and utter contempt for the medical system; and tales
of her 'gorgeous' handpainted panhandling sign when she was
begging on the street. Her tone was frighteningly matter-of-fact,
and every word struck straight into my heart. Through all that
pathetic recital, my mind kept asking the unanswerable: Why?
Why had she not come home? Why had she persisted in living
such a life when she must have known I was trying to find her?
I did not dare to give voice to those queries for fear that
Margaret would see them as judgemental.

Worst of all was the unreal feeling that this was a stranger
I was listening to – a woman I did not know. Truth to tell, I
had not really known her for several years. Poor Jenny was in
bits.

Chapter Seventeen

As has been true so many times in the past, I did exactly the *wrong* thing – I simply did not realize just how fragile Margaret's health was. She could walk for only a limited time, and after choosing two outfits (including two baggy tops to hide those pitiful bones), she went outside the shop and sat propped up against the wall.

For lunch, she suggested a huge Food Centre in the mall – 15 or 20 fast food shops, noisy, frantic with movement. She had trouble eating, and only picked at her Chinese food (apparently a favourite cuisine). True to her street lifestyle, she insisted on packing the remainder in her big shoulder bag (which seemed to be a security symbol, since she didn't let go of it, even in the motel room) to take back to the motel. I managed to convince her I should carry the paper bag of food myself when it started leaking, and when Jenny and I were on our own in the shops, while Margaret waited outside, I simply discarded it and told her that the bag had got so soggy that it had broken.

During our entire stay in that shopping mall, I was very conscious of the disapproving looks that her appearance generated, and I wondered if she noticed them. She had said several times that she was embarrassed at not being properly dressed, but that was obviously an embarrassment at what she thought *I* felt – I prayed a silent prayer that she would be oblivious to the reactions of other shoppers. I'm pretty sure Jenny was keenly aware of it, although neither of us mentioned it, and certainly neither Jenny nor I felt any embarrassment, only compassion that she had come to such a state.

When we returned to the motel, Margaret took a hot bath (God only knows when she had last had access to a real bathroom!) and went to bed, where she stayed the rest of the afternoon and night.

The motel had a 24-hour coffee shop/restaurant on the grounds which turned into a real refuge for Jenny and I. It would have been an even greater Godsend if the air conditioning hadn't been broken. Going over for meals or a short break to get out of that awful room was something of an ordeal in the stifling heat, even though the very kind owner usually moved the fan over to blow directly on us.

26 August 1995

Tonight, Jenny and I took Margaret a hamburger, salad, and French fries. After nibbling at them half-heartedly, she promptly went into the bathroom and vomited it all back up. I know she needs a lot of food, but how on earth am I going to get any into her? She has always been picky about what she will eat, and now not even the things she likes will stay down.

I wonder if it is really too late for her and that we will lose her before too much longer. Sleep will not come easily this night, even though I feel totally drained, emotionally and physically.

27 August 1995

Woke from a restless, largely sleepless night. Jenny lay on her stomach and never moved all night, although I know she was awake a good bit of the time. She must be worried about losing the remaining foetus, since light bleeding has come on since we left Ireland. I wonder if she is having pain as well. No good trying to talk to her, though.

Sarah called to say that an application for disability Social Security benefits was filed for Margaret when she was released from hospital on 10 August, and gave me a number and name to call to find out if it can be expedited, since it takes two-and-a-half to three months to get through the bureaucracy. When I talked to Elizabeth on the telephone, she insisted she will drive to Austin and take Margaret back to Columbia to stay with her, but because of her own financial situation, she cannot manage it until Margaret's Social Security payments begin.

With all the problems Margaret has caused her so many times in the past, it is incredible that she should feel so strongly about taking this on. I can't help but worry about her as well as Margaret.

When I asked Margaret how she felt about going with

Elizabeth, with a grim expression she replied, 'I have no choice, do I?' She repeated that all through the day, always with the same grimness. It seemed to me that she had been really frightened by her physical condition – but for that, she would probably never have tried to reach us. There was also a real probability that she might disappear again if she regained enough strength.

My own finances were melting like ice in the 100-degree heat, which meant I would have to find a safe place for Margaret to stay until Elizabeth could come for her. One certainty overshadowed everything else: I could not possibly leave Austin without some sort of shelter for Margaret. Where to start looking? Once more, I called on Sarah, and she gave me a few agency names that may be able to help.

27 August 1995 (Continuation)
This entire day has been spent on the telephone – and because it is Sunday, I had great difficulty in getting hold of anyone. The Salvation Army seemed the best starting place, even though Margaret insists she won't go there because 'they are so mean and they won't let you stay in bed'. Still, it's the only hostel for the homeless in Austin. And there was a man on duty to answer the phone, but without a doubt, he was a rude and unhelpful person. His rote answer to every question was 'there's no one here until tomorrow'. He refused to take a message, and had only his stock reply when I lost patience and exploded, telling him that I knew the Salvation Army was there to help in emergencies, and not to put urgent situations on hold. Maybe I've been too long in Ireland, where people bend rules every day of the week to help someone in trouble.

After calling the Red Cross, the Federal Office of Housing and Homeless Problems, Blackland Transitional Housing, Casa Marianella, Capita, the Community Partnership for the Homeless, the Lutheran Diocese Social Services, and HOBO (Brothers of the Homeless – can't remember the proper full name); leaving messages on answering machines, and talking to one or two real people who turned me down flat, I finally gave up in despair.

My homesickness for Ireland and Cappoquin just got more and more acute with every call, which is probably what prompted the notion that if I could just find one Irish-born person, I'd get some help. So, Jenny and I took ourselves over to the coffee shop and went through the city telephone directory looking for anything listed under 'Irish' – not a single entry!! So, we started through the yellow pages, looking for Catholic Agencies. Back to the telephone to call the St Louis Catholic Church emergency number and Our Lady's Marionite Catholic Church, leaving messages on both answering machines. As a last resort, I called the Diocese of Austin emergency number and finally talked to a real live person. She, however, cannot reach the person who may be able to help until tomorrow afternoon.

It just seems hopeless, and I don't know what I am going to do. There is no way I can pay for her to stay in a motel, and unless some of those answering machine messages yield something tomorrow, I just may panic – have been trying all day to hold it together and get the practicalities taken care of before the money gives out completely and we have to leave.

I had been avoiding an actual count of the money left, but it just could not be avoided any longer. Two more days at the most, so I took a deep breath and, with my heart in my throat, announced that Jenny and I would have to go home on Tuesday. I knew I could not leave Margaret stranded, but I was hoping against hope that we would find a temporary home for her.

Once the decision was made, I called four of the airlines that serve Austin/NYC, and was shocked to find that the one-way fare for one without prior booking was a whopping $547. Jenny, bless her, immediately insisted that we go by Amtrak, the U.S. rail system – no problem for me, since I enjoy train travel. But it was another shock to find that the trip takes three days Austin/Chicago/ NYC), and with Jenny's continual bleeding I worried about such strenuous travel. However, the fare for us both, with reserved coach seats, was only a little over $400, so I went ahead and booked us for Tuesday, charging it to the American Express card, which was already groaning from the expense of this trip.

God alone knew what the next day would bring – I would just have to start again trying to reach *someone* who could help.

28 August 1995

Very frustrating morning – I didn't dare use the telephone in case there were call-backs from all those answering machine messages. Nothing by lunchtime, and panic was creeping up on me. Jenny went for takeaway lunches for us, and while we were eating it, the phone rang and I positively jumped at it. It was Elizabeth, who said she was borrowing the money and coming for Margaret right away. Since disability payments are Federal, she will pursue Margaret's application from Columbia. It's a two-day drive, and she will leave tomorrow morning, so that means we only have to find shelter for Margaret for three days.

My heart is so full of love and appreciation for my oldest daughter. Elizabeth's basic instincts are all I would want them to be, and it is wonderful to know that she is anxious to share this awful responsibility for Margaret. It's such a heavy one, and since making this trip, I have wondered if I really am up to shouldering it alone any longer.

We called Sarah and Anne Richards (a freelance editor who lives alone and has befriended Margaret for several years) to let them know the situation, and I was getting ready to call Salvation Army again to see if they would take Margaret for the three days, when the phone rang, and it was Anne, who said she would be glad to have her until Elizabeth gets here. Immediately after her call, the Catholic Diocese office called back from my message yesterday – the only call-back all day! Thank God for Anne's offer, which Margaret seems to welcome. We rang Sarah, and since our train leaves at 9:45a.m. in the morning, she will come after work to take Margaret over to Anne's.

It is impossible to describe the enormity of the relief that swept over Jenny and I, but I tried to conceal my relief from Margaret, who might well have misinterpreted it. Again, Jenny knew just what to do. 'Granny,' she said when we were out for a smoke, 'we both need a drink and to get out of here for a break.' So, on the pretext of going for cigarettes, she and I took a taxi to a nearby Mexican restaurant and had two quick drinks before heading back to the motel. Lifesaving!

Later that day I had an extraordinary telephone call from my sister Louise. She was ringing to say that my 83 year-old aunt, Lee, who lived in Washington, DC, wanted to wire me $500 to help with expenses, so I asked her to arrange to send $300 to Elizabeth and $200 to me in NYC. All my life I had felt a special bond with Lee, and this understanding of the practical problems I now faced made her even more dear to me. I was simply not up to talking to anyone at that moment, but before leaving for Ireland, I would call from New York and try to tell her (as well as her husband, Carl) just how much they both meant to me.

Sarah arrived about 10 p.m., and we all went over to Anne's house – I wanted to meet her and thank her personally. Margaret seemed to be content to be left there, and as Sarah drove us back to the motel, she wanted to take us to see Margaret's abandoned car 'home'. I just can't express the dread I felt at that prospect, or the hurtful images that overwhelmed me when I saw that junkyard and thought of Margaret – or *anyone* – living here, or dark nights that must have been frightening, and cold weather with no heat. Tears simply could not be held back, and poor Jenny was in bits, openly crying in the back seat. It was probably the most heartbreaking incident in this whole sad trip.

Jenny (now bleeding profusely) and I packed and fell into bed. Our hearts were so full that neither of us could talk much, and I really wanted to put my arms around her and try to comfort her – and myself.

Chapter Seventeen

29 August 1995

Our 9:45a.m. train finally arrived at 2p.m.! Four long hours in the searing heat. Amtrak confirmed my lifelong affection when the station master sent out for pizza and soft drinks for all us poor, sweltering passengers.

Our seats are really quite comfortable, and we managed to get to sleep. As we get farther and farther away from Austin, a sort of dread seems to be building inside my head – Margaret's illness has been so devastating to those who have tried to help her in the past – there's no use denying that she could very well wreck Elizabeth's hard-won life style.

30–31 August 1995

Finally reached Chicago, with only about two hours' wait before our connection to NYC, instead of the original six hours. My emotional control was at the breaking point, as was Jenny's, and for about a half-hour we were at cross purposes, one of the few times in all these years we've had a falling out.

When our train was finally announced, we filed out to the platform, only to learn that despite our reserved tickets, the train was filled with passengers from another train that had been running almost a day late. My exhaustion was complete, both physical and emotional.

We had been in the holding lounge only a few minutes when an Amtrak official announced that any passengers who were willing to sit in the lounge car for the 22-hour trip could board the train. I was on my feet before he even finished – I was willing to do anything to get underway on this last leg. Little did I know what an agony it was to be! Hard-backed chairs and a group of thoroughly obnoxious people, most of whom had left reserved seats to travel in the lounge car, who caroused all night long, making it impossible to snatch a little sleep. Dreadful night and early morning. It wasn't until we reached New York that Jenny confided that during the nightmarish journey she had lost the second twin foetus. A terrible blow to her already tattered emotions! My heart broke for her.

Never had I been so glad to see Michael, who was waiting for us in New York. Even before unpacking for our brief stay with him, I booked our flight back to Ireland for Sunday, 3 September, arriving early Monday morning at Shannon.

1 September 1995

To my dismay, every time I try to talk to Michael about Margaret and Elizabeth and the whole Austin trip, my throat chokes up and tears run down my cheeks. Would that it were a release!

All through the next two long, lazy days at home with Michael and Jenny, tears were still bedeviling me. I would have closed a door and cried them all out if I had thought it would help.

Monday, 4 September 1995

During our flight back to Ireland, Jenny and I relived that awful Austin trip, and in the course of remembering the drive to see where Margaret had been living in an abandoned car, Jenny said something that touched me deeply. 'Granny,' she said, 'it really broke my heart to think of my mother living like that, but I can't imagine how much worse it would be if it were my child. It must have been really awful for you.'

When I tried to tell her how very sorry I felt about her mother's condition, she turned around and said, 'Let's face it, Granny – you have always been my mother'.

Even though I have always tried to keep alive for her the fact that it is Margaret who is her mother and that only her illness has kept her apart from us, I will treasure that heartfelt sentiment for the rest of my life.

When we arrived at Shannon Airport, Jenny and Seán were almost pathetically happy to be together again – I hadn't realized before that this is their very first separation since they were married. The drive home to Cappoquin seemed much too long, although the wonderful scenery all along the way was a balm to my soul, which is only now beginning to tell me how deeply it has been wounded.

Chapter Seventeen

My own fireside never looked so good. The little house only lacks Michael, and I pray to God he'll be able to come over to stay next year.

And Now…

A little over two years have passed since that traumatic trip to Austin. In the best of all possible worlds, I would be able to look back and see that as the beginning of a new life for Margaret, surrounded by loving family, her physical needs watched over, and Elizabeth's professional expertise to help her cope with her emotional troubles. How I wish that were the case! It isn't.

In the early days of her stay in South Carolina with Elizabeth, Margaret responded well to her surroundings and soon began gaining weight. She slept the days away, often staying awake watching television through the night until 6 a.m. She refused to sleep on Elizabeth's sofa/bed, but stretched out on blankets she laid on the floor behind one of the larger chairs. Elizabeth and I both felt this was part of a residue of her long years in that abandoned car – as she became more accustomed to a more normal way of life we felt she would move to the bed.

After about three weeks, a long letter (seven handwritten pages) from Elizabeth held more insight into many of Margaret's problems than I had been able to glean from all my contacts with doctors and all the reading I had done over the years. With her intimate knowledge of our family background, as well as her professional training, she shed a bright light of understanding on the bewilderment that had spawned so much of my emotional anguish.

28 September 1995

Excerpts from Elizabeth's letter

I think that as a child, Margaret never really bonded with you or anyone else. Just a part of her emotional makeup, nobody's fault. She seems to have bonded with me to the extent that she was able, though I didn't really bond with her at that time. She always felt emotionally blank to me in some way. I didn't think about those things as a child, but it's clear to me now that Margaret took a few instances of closeness here and there and exaggerated them in her mind into a viable sibling closeness. I don't try to contradict that part of her memory.

She has a phenomenal memory for past events, even when she was a toddler, but she gets times mixed up and understands almost none of the motivation of people around her.

I can't just categorically challenge Margaret's memory or her interpretations. She has a very deep mindset that she hasn't ever been mentally ill. She won't even acknowledge known statistics that at least one-third of the homeless are mentally ill and need help to get disability payments and other help. She is vehement in that. I don't see any sign of mental illness in her now, though I'm not sure that her persistent use of her radio headset, even when she wakes briefly, isn't to ward off voices or other sorts of turmoil. I doubt we'll ever know about that. I have told her a little about why she was considered mentally ill, why you kept taking her to hospitals, and I'll continue to do so a little at a time when it comes up.

The medications doctors have used with her have such horrifying effects (they really do) that any suggestion of a mental disorder scares the shit out of her. She is far from alone in that – a lot of mental patients have learned to say that they are 'allergic' to whatever drugs are problems for them. I can't tell you what it feels like to take some of those drugs – it's almost impossible to describe the hellish torment of them even while they make you look fine on the outside.

She responds well to comments about how well she survived her ten years on the street and how easily she made friends, etc. Margaret does have a warm and generous nature that isn't totally superficial, but I think with family her defences are up because she doesn't remember a lot about her past. We have talked about it a lot, and she could look back and see the connections there and understand why she stayed in the lockup overnight and that the judge had suggested you do that – why you were worried enough to react that extremely. It will take a long time to help Margaret to see things in the way they were intended, but I'm slowly working on it.

Her refusal of the mental illness thing is, I think, a very normal protective process and one with survival value. I just hope over time to help her see her life and others in a way that makes sense and allows her to make real emotional connections with people. That will be a slow process, as I said, but I think that Margaret could develop an appropriate closeness with you with some positive feedback from you.

I think that the way society judges parents – especially when we were children – forced you into a defensive frame of mind regarding both of us, and that wasn't justified then or now. You don't have to explain anything or defend anything or punish yourself. You really were a very good parent in many ways. Margaret's distancing herself was caused by things beyond your control and unrelated to you. I still feel close to you, but sometimes your defensiveness makes it difficult to show it.

One thing is crystal clear – Margaret deeply needs your genuine approval in small enough doses not to overwhelm her. I don't think you can give it if you stay defensive, overly worried about who we think is at fault. You need to stop worrying about how she sees you from the past and concentrate on giving her positive feedback and lots of love now. It meant wonders to Margaret that you and Jenny came to Austin, and so quickly. And that I came. She's starting to get used to the idea that she really is welcome here and that her family really cares and wants her as part of it.

The people of Austin – so many who befriended and looked out for her – have greatly helped in her healing, as will others here. And I hope I can be part of that, and you and Jenny as well.

One thing that has come out in our talks is that Margaret hitchhiked all over the country with truckers for three years. Only three approached her sexually, the rest just appreciated the company. She was in a serious accident in another part of South Carolina during that time. One shoulder was pulled completely apart, the other arm hurt somehow. It was pretty bad. Anyway, she's been very fortunate in a lot of ways, and somehow protected, but I hope she begins to understand how lucky she was not to be hurt seriously.

How much unnecessary pain could have been avoided had even one of Margaret's numerous doctors talked to me in such a vein!

Elizabeth began setting in motion Margaret's application for federal disability benefits, which would take months for approval, but which, if approved, would allow her the independence of a place of her own. She also helped Margaret obtain the food stamps that went a long way towards paying for groceries.

By mid-October, however, Margaret's behaviour was a source of serious concern for Elizabeth. One letter from her explains: 'Margaret has been acting fine until recently, when she has been spending hours away from here on a street that is infested with drugs and prostitution. Her personality has started going suddenly crazy. She will be fine for hours, then suddenly weird. I know she is drinking when she is away from the apartment, and she may be on drugs. I don't think she will ever leave the stuff alone. She doesn't want to. Her doctor in Texas was aiding her in her drinking by referring to it as 'maintenance drinking', as though that level was all right. But any member of AA will tell you that what people own up to is only the half of it.'

By the end of November, Elizabeth had been completely shut out of any closeness with Margaret, who became more and more paranoid and manipulative and finally moved out, telling Elizabeth she was going to a hostel run by a local religious group to stay until her benefit cheques began arriving. When I rang there, however, they informed me that Margaret was not there and had never been there.

25 November 1995

I feel so alone, and don't know what I can do, or if there is anything I can do to find her. Will she disappear for another eight years? So many times in the past I've felt like this! Yet I had really forgotten the total devastation.

When I talked to Elizabeth tonight, I tried to tell her how very sorry I am for this major disruption of her own life and that I should never have permitted her to come for Margaret. 'No, Mama,' she said, 'it has served a purpose – Margaret will now have her disability benefits, so she won't be penniless, and she has food stamps, and she has had enough rest now to regain some strength, so we don't have to worry about her quite so much.' All that is directly due to Elizabeth's running around, taking Margaret to the proper agencies, and insisting that she get some help. No bitterness at all. My heart just filled to overflowing.

That same heart will never, I think, heal from the pain I feel for Margaret, but at the same time, both Jenny and I realize that there is really nothing we can do to help her. How sad for her, even more than for us, that she told me on the phone, 'You bitch, you always take up for that other bitch. I don't even want to remember that Elizabeth is my sister'. The truth is, I don't think there is much doubt that she would probably be dead by now without Elizabeth's rescue.

There is very little left of the sweet – and charming – Margaret we once knew, and we are going to have to be resigned to letting her go, with our prayers that she will be able to continue to survive in whatever way she follows. I had hoped that being with family would be healing for her, but it just isn't to be. Such a waste! But she absolutely refuses to recognize her illness and accept treatment, and there doesn't seem to be any way to persuade her.

When next we heard from Margaret, she was back in Austin. A Catholic charity was paying for her apartment, and Sarah McCoy's AA friends and church prayer group were helping her with furniture and living expenses. When rent on that apartment rose beyond the means of the charity organization, Margaret stayed in the Salvation Army hostel in Austin until the summer of 1996, when she was given a much nicer apartment by the Texas Housing Authority. She was also given a bus pass that allows her much more freedom of movement.

1 July 1996

Excerpt from letter from Margaret
Dear Mama,

When I had to face the fact that I could no longer function normally, far from it, it hurt terribly. It still does. I can now fully understand how bad Poppie [my father] hurt inside in Florida when he could no longer do what he had been able to do all his life. Every night out in that field, I would have to face the fact that I was now dysfunctional and realize how badly I needed some help to get somewhere I could manage by myself without being in a nursing home. I thought 'I really need help so badly I'll even pray. I need help from anyone.' And so it has come.

I think of Jenny a lot more than she knows and want so that her life with Seán will be perfect. Please give them my love. I show the pictures of them and those gorgeous rosy cheeked Irish grandchildren every chance I get.

Mama, you'll never know how many, many times I have thanked God for having had you for a mother. Without you, I don't think I would have ever survived the last fifty years (almost fifty). You are truly one in a million. There aren't enough words in the English language to tell you how much I've loved you all these years.

Please give everyone my love, and I'll write again when I can.

I love you,
Margaret

Tears would not be held back when I read this long (three pages) letter. Even more than the relief of knowing that she was in a safe and secure place, her recognition of the fact that she would always need help and went straight to my heart. This letter came closest to the kind of honest communication we had shared in her childhood than any other. It had been years since I felt our contacts went beyond the superficial. Remembering Elizabeth's analysis of my own emotional shortcomings, I could now put aside the defensiveness that had stood between us in the past and believe that her protestations of love were genuine.

Does this recognition of her physical needs mean that she is at long last ready to face her emotional problems? Will she seek the medication and treatment she has so desperately needed in the past? Will she be able, with all the help she now has, to sustain the comfortable lifestyle that has been so hard won? Or will the demons of her illness yet again drive her to the streets? Before her story ends, will she gradually slip into the role of a pitiful burned-out schizophrenic like so many others who wander the streets of cities all over the world? I don't know.

Whatever lies ahead for her, I have faced the immeasurably sad certainty that our lives will forever be apart from one another, the inescapable acknowledgement that, whether because of her illness or other reasons I cannot fathom, Margaret simply does not want me – or Jenny – in her life. I must be content in the knowledge that so many people are looking after her in a way I have never been, and never will be, able to. Still, the heartache will not go away, and at times is overwhelming. It is then that I look at Jenny, and I know there will always be a part of my daughter in my life.

I once heard an interview on Ireland's national radio station with the mother of a schizophrenic child in which she said, 'When schizophrenia hits your child, you will never, never, *never* accept it – you will just get on with it.' She is dead right. Nor do guilt and anger ever completely disappear. But I have learned that, even though acceptance is impossible, indeed intolerable, mothers of schizophrenic children can, and must, make the necessary *adjustments* in our own inner lives that will underpin the strength we need time after time to cope with the acute psychotic episodes that afflict our children.

We must just get on with it as best we can.

Epilogue

Margaret died in the early hours of 10 January 1998 and is buried in the Travis County International Cemetery in Austin, Texas.

I could not be with her, but the day before her death, we had a telephone conversation I shall treasure all my life. She was in a great deal of pain, but quite lucid, and I could ask her if she were frightened. Her honest reply came from the Margaret I knew so many years ago – 'I am more frightened of not being able to do things for myself, Mama. I don't want to live that way.'

I do feel she was reassured and comforted when I told her I'd be there holding her hand, just as when she was a child and scared about having her tonsils removed. I had told her back then that I'd be right there holding her hand in the operating room even though they stopped me at the door. Her last words to me were a soft, heartfelt 'I love you, Mama, I always have'. With her last breath she asked the hospice nurse to hold her hand, and I hope with all my heart that she felt it was my hand clasping hers.